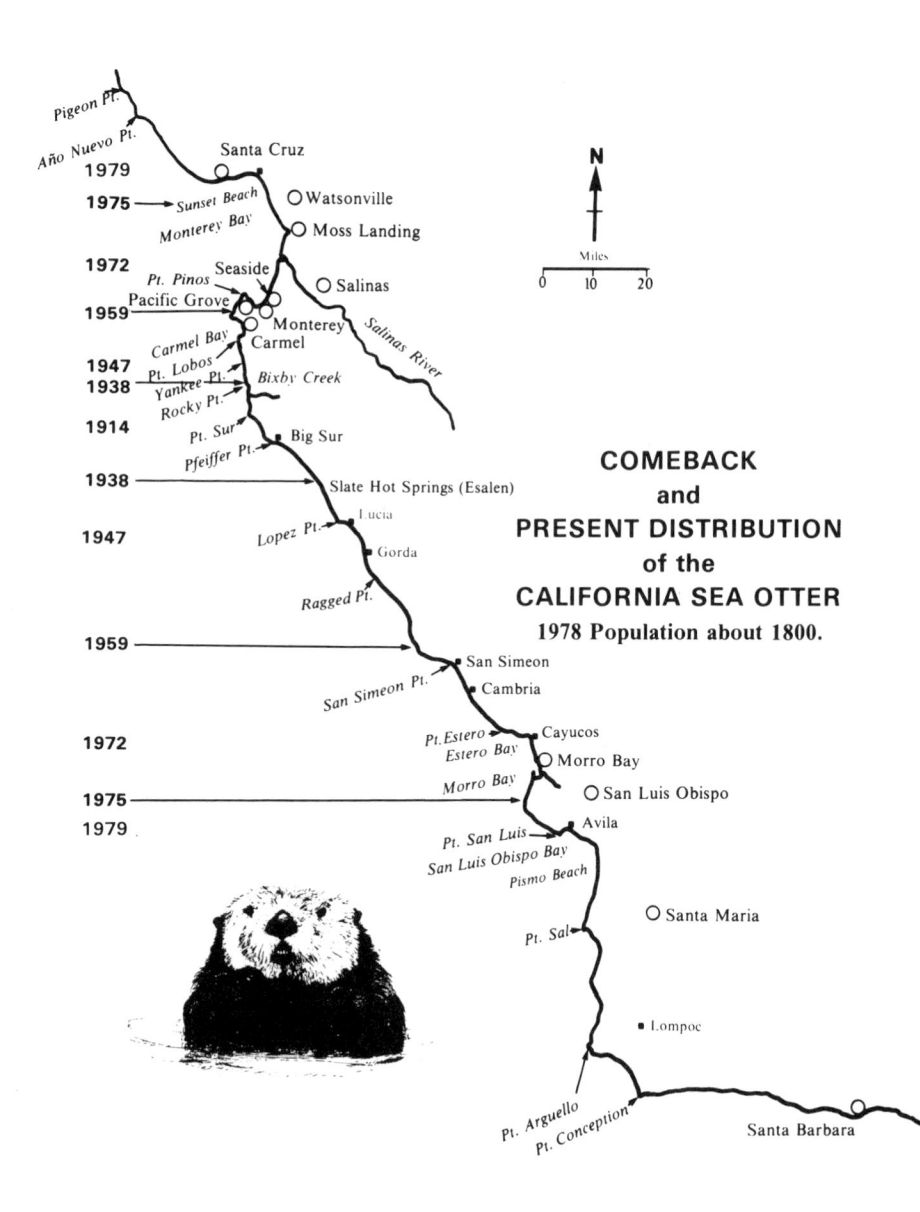

Pigeon Pt.

Año Nuevo Pt.
1979

Santa Cruz

1975 → Sunset Beach
Monterey Bay

○ Watsonville

○ Moss Landing

1972   Seaside
Pt. Pinos
Pacific Grove
1959

○ Salinas

○ Monterey
Carmel Bay   Carmel
1947   Pt. Lobos
1938   Yankee Pt.   Bixby Creek
Rocky Pt.

Salinas River

1914
Pt. Sur   Big Sur
Pfeiffer Pt.

1938 ───────────→ Slate Hot Springs (Esalen)

Lucia
1947   Lopez Pt.
Gorda

Ragged Pt.

1959 ──────────────────→ San Simeon
Cambria
San Simeon Pt.

1972   Pt. Estero ─→ Cayucos
Estero Bay   ○ Morro Bay
1975 ─────────── Morro Bay
1979   ○ San Luis Obispo
Avila
Pt. San Luis
San Luis Obispo Bay
Pismo Beach

○ Santa Maria

Pt. Sal

▪ Lompoc

Pt. Arguello
Pt. Conception   Santa Barbara ○

N

Miles

0   10   20

COMEBACK
and
PRESENT DISTRIBUTION
of the
CALIFORNIA SEA OTTER

1978 Population about 1800.

The sea otter's long lustrous fur has always been a matter of life and death for the only marine mammal without a thick layer of fat under the skin. With the coming of Europeans into Pacific waters, both Alaskan and California sea otters were brought to near-extinction by hunters seeking the most fabulous fur they had ever seen. It has been illegal since 1911 to kill sea otters in the North Pacific and in California without a permit. Despite the many years of protection by the U.S. government, sea otters in California numbered only about 1,800 animals in a 1976 census, a small proportion of the 16,000 or more that once floated and fed in and near the kelp beds along California shores. Now the sea otter is again threatened precisely because of its extraordinary fur. Sea otter fur and spilled oil do mix, but the result is dead sea otters. A single massive oil spill could mean extinction for an animal so vulnerable and with so limited a range. (R. Coulter)

THE
CALIFORNIA
SEA OTTER

Saved or Doomed?

by

John Woolfenden

THE BOXWOOD PRESS

Distributed by:

The Boxwood Press
P.O. Box 444
Pacific Grove, CA 93950

408—375-9110

ISBN: 0-910286-52-3

Printed in U.S.A.

PREFACE

SOME TIME in the late spring or early summer of 1977, Dr. Ralph Buchsbaum invited me to write a book on sea otters, to be published by the Boxwood Press.

Why me?

Well, as reporter, feature writer, columnist, and finally Sunday editor of the *Monterey Peninsula Herald,* I had met and interviewed and knew personally virtually everyone connected with sea otter research on the central California coast. I had written about these people for *The Herald* and its *Weekend Magazine.* I believed the otters to be delightful, enchanting, highly intelligent creatures deserving of as complete a written presentation as possible. And Dr. Buchsbaum believed that I could do an impartial job of it.

By September 1977, I had a first draft ready. But whoever said that books aren't written, they are rewritten, was understating the case.

With Dr. Betty Davis, zoologist and parasitologist at the University of California's Hastings Natural History Reservation, I went over and over the manuscript. She provided additional material, some from her own writings; suggested additional reading, brought me up-to-date on new discoveries, as did her husband, Dr. John Davis, vertebrate zoologist and director of Hastings.

At the California Department of Fish and Game, I became reacquainted with Dan Miller, Dick Burge, Earl Ebert, Paul Wilde, and Jack Ames, all of whom I had known in previous years and all of whom gave unstintingly of their time, their official records, their personal opinions, as did Ron Jameson of the U.S. Fish and Wildlife Service.

Jud Vandevere, research specialist for the Friends of the Sea Otter, went over my script at least twice, told me in great detail of his own observations.

Those underwater camera experts, Bill Bryan and Dr. Jim Mattison, regaled me with tales of their adventures and brought examples of their photographic work.

I am indebted to Margaret Owings, president of the Friends of the Sea Otter, for permitting me to excerpt material from the Friends' publication, *The Otter Raft,* and for providing her own account of the battle to insure protection of the sea otters; to W. R. Holman of Pacific Grove, for his stories about a shoreline paved with abalones; to Dr. John Pearse of the University of California, Santa Cruz, who came from a diving expedition with his class, to read my manuscript and offer suggestions; to Dr. Tom Williams, veterinarian, who added research data; and to Ralph and Mildred Buchsbaum, who rearranged the text to greater advantage, checked and rechecked every statement, obtained the needed illustrations, and smoothed over my irascibility when I was sure that the book would never reach the bookstores during my lifetime, due to constantly changing attitudes by governmental bodies on such matters as otter "management," offshore drilling, tanker traffic, and other threats to otter peace and security, on all of which we wanted to be up-to-date.

If I have omitted the name or names of anyone else who aided me, it was unintentional. They will probably find themselves mentioned in the text.

I should like to express special thanks to my wife, Elizabeth, who has read proof constantly, on the original and every revision, until she knows it all by heart and could recite it more expertly than I.

J. R. W.

Carmel Valley, California

CONTENTS

Large adult male eating a clam without first breaking it open on a rock held on the chest. A forepaw is pushing the clam into the mouth, where the heavy shells will be crushed into pieces between large flattened molars powered by strong jaw muscles. (R. Buchsbaum)

1

CLOWNS OF THE KELP

A TELEVISION CAMERA covering the annual Bing Crosby golf tournament at Pebble Beach, California, suddenly swung away from the action to show a view of the surface of nearby Stillwater Cove. There a sea otter was floating on its back, paddling leisurely with its hind flippers while holding a juicy morsel of shellfish in its forepaws and munching happily away, oblivious of the crowds on the fairways above.

The cameraman, probably given a nudge by some network official to get back to the business of golf, returned rapidly to tee and green, while thousands of viewers lamented the fact that their glimpse of the otter had been all too hasty.

In the same Stillwater Cove, Jacques Cousteau and his son Philippe photographed much of the footage of their highly popular television film, *The Unsinkable Sea Otter.* Probably no animal other than the koala bear has captured the public imagination so completely as this "teddy bear of the ocean."

It looks cute. It looks almost cuddly. It looks friendly, and inquisitive, and intelligent. As it bobs up out of the kelp, glances quickly to see what's happening around it, then disappears below the surface, the viewer expects to hear it say, in the words of the White Rabbit in *Alice in Wonderland,* "Oh, my fur and whiskers!"

A scuba diver off Monterey's Cannery Row was amazed when one of the animals swam towards him, reached out a paw and touched his faceplate, then looked through the glass to check further on this unfamiliar animal invading its territory. Thinking that this was a friendly gesture, the scuba diver reached out in similar fashion, intending to stroke the otter's fur, but pulled back his hand in a hurry, having been nipped by the otter's teeth. "Cute all right, but certainly not cuddly," was the diver's verdict.

1

Close encounters of the otter kind. Scuba diver and sea otter surface simultaneously in Monterey Bay and consider whether to investigate each other further. (J. A. Mattison, Jr.)

There are few more delightful experiences, however, than to see a mother sea otter place her pup in strands of the giant kelp, *Macrocystis,* just before she dives for food for the two of them. This will hold the youngster in place until she returns. But if the mother is gone too long, it may cry like a kitten or a human baby, until she reappears.

Enhydra lutris nereis, to give the southern sea otter its scientific name, is the smallest marine mammal in the oceans of the world but the largest member, in the northern hemisphere, of the family Mustelidae, which includes the river otters, ermines, fishers, weasels, minks, wolverines, badgers, skunks, and martens. It is believed to have evolved from a river otterlike ancestor. Its body, like the bodies of all marine mammals, has slowly increased in size, an adaptation to the high heat loss it has experienced in cold water. Fully grown male sea otters measure about four and a half feet long and average 58 pounds, though the heaviest one handled on the central California coast weighed 87 pounds. Adult females average about 41 pounds. While buoyancy of the sea water has supported an increasingly large body, the legs have slowly shortened or become modified for swimming and holding rather than walking.

2

The North American river otter, *Lutra canadensis,* resembles its marine relative. Both have long sinuous bodies, short limbs, and webbed feet—all adaptations to aquatic life in animals descended from land carnivores. Though sea otters are almost entirely aquatic, river otters spend more of their time outside water than in. They are often seen crossing quiet roads in forests, and can make long overland treks, but when alarmed retreat to water. In rivers, lakes, or swamps they feed on fishes, crayfishes, frogs, snails, and any small birds or rodents they can catch. Otters that live near sea coasts may enter marine waters and feed there, sometimes being mistaken for sea otters. Conversely, sea otters have been maintained in a Seattle zoo in a pool of running fresh water, but as zoo exhibits they are less adaptable than the river otters. In nature these last seem to take special pleasure in repeatedly sliding down mud and snow banks; and when they are provided, in zoos, with a steep slide heading into a pool they put on a great show.

River and land otters (of several genera) live on every continent except Australia. The largest of otters is probably the giant otter *(Pteroneura brasiliensis)* of the great river systems of South America, in which males have been reported to reach over 7 feet. (R. Buchsbaum)

Captive northern sea otter walking on all fours around the edge of an enclosed tank at Prince William Sound, Alaska. (D. Costa)

Onshore, when they have "hauled out" onto a sandy beach or a rocky promontory, southern sea otters may appear almost awkward. They can make progress by planting the forefeet, either together or alternately, in a forward position, then swiveling or pulling the rear end along. They may hop, using forefeet and hind flippers alternately, or may walk with alternate steps, like river otters. Alaskan sea otters, according to observers, are more in the habit of bending the body into a U-shape and walking on all fours.

California sea otter walking on the beach behind Hopkins Marine Station in Pacific Grove, on Monterey Bay. Named "Hopkins," this sea otter hauled out regularly, for 18 months, to spend the night sleeping on this protected beach. (A. Baldridge)

Perhaps because they live in habitats relatively undisturbed by humans, and because of rougher seas in the north, Alaskan sea otters haul out on land frequently, sometimes more than a hundred in a group. The California otters are much less prone to haul out, but as many as 23 have been seen together at Cypress Point on the Monterey Peninsula.

Hauling out was less rare in the past, if we are to judge from old accounts such as that of Comte J. F. G. de La Pérouse, a Frenchman who in 1786 commanded the first non-Spanish expedition to visit Monterey Bay. Though the two frigates under La Pérouse later disappeared in the south Pacific, his journal had already been sent home on another ship. An English edition of the journal, translated and edited by M. L. A. Milet-Mureau, was published in 1798. La Pérouse objected to what he saw as violation of the rights of the Indians at Carmel Mission; and among his observations on Indian life and skills, he had this to say about the killing of otters that hauled out in the Monterey Bay area:

> The Indians, who are not so good seamen as the Esquimaux, and whose boats at Monterey are only made of reeds, catch them on land with snares, or by knocking them down with large sticks when they find them at a distance from the shore; for this purpose, they keep themselves concealed behind rocks, for this animal is frightened at the least noise, and immediately plunges into the water.

Presumably, those otters who failed to be frightened at the approach of humans left fewer descendants. This suggests how, through natural selection, a large and genetically varied population adapts, over long periods of time, to hazards and to changing environments. It also reminds us that the modern California population of sea otters, all derived from a small and highly inbred remnant of an originally large population, may have lost much of their genetic variability. This could make them especially vulnerable to changing conditions, just when human disturbances and pollution are occurring at a greatly accelerated rate.

In the water otters are all in their element, swimming, floating, rolling, somersaulting, twisting, diving, maneuvering with consummate skill and agility, and seeming to enjoy every minute of it.

If you have watched an otter feeding, you have probably noticed that it rolls over in the water from time to time. This washes away food particles which otherwise might become embedded in the fur, and also picks up the air bubbles required by the undercoat. Subjected to an oil spill, or even to the small amounts of oil that escape from the ordinary uses of boats—an increasingly dangerous threat due to the growth of tanker traffic—the fur would become matted, the undercoat useless, cold water would penetrate to the skin, and the animal would chill and die.

In an Environmental Impact Report prepared for Lower Cook Inlet, Alaska, the statement was made that "... it appears that exposure to relatively small amounts of refined fuels and/or crude oil will cause death."

ORIGINALLY the sea otter range extended from the northern coast of Japan, across the Bering Sea to Alaska, and down the Pacific Coast as far as Baja California. Commercial hunting, at first primarily by Russians with Aleut crews, reduced the animals to a tiny fraction of their original numbers. The pelts, treasured at the Imperial Russian court and equally prized by wealthy, high-ranking Chinese, brought a high price in the marketplace. Only when it became too expensive to hunt the few that were left, did the Russians, in 1841, abandon their outposts at Fort Ross and Bodega Bay in what was then Mexican Alta California.

THOUGH the otters staged a comeback in Alaskan waters, they were believed extinct along the California coast for many years. Actually, a few ranchers along the Big Sur coastline, and members of the U.S. Coast Guard's lighthouse crew at Point Sur, knew that there was a small herd, of perhaps 14, in that vicinity during the early 1900s, but agreed to keep quiet about it lest the

A historic picture. Taken by William L. Morgan off the mouth of Bixby Creek in April 1938, this is the photograph which confirmed the fact that "rafting" otters had been seen there the previous month by Mr. and Mrs. Howard G. Sharpe, and which proved that the animal, believed by many to be extinct, was staging a comeback on the central California coast. (Monterey Public Library)

animals be hunted once more. Then in March 1938, Mr. and Mrs. Howard G. Sharpe, who resided near Bixby Creek bridge, about 15 miles south of Carmel, reported seeing what looked like "a couple of hundred" rafting otters in the ocean near the mouth of the creek. Dr. Rolf Bolin of Stanford University's Hopkins Marine Station admitted to "raised eyebrows" at this large number estimated, but on March 25 confirmed that there were "about 50." In April, William Morgan of Monterey lowered himself down the cliffs to photograph them.

Dr. Harold Heath, a colleague of Bolin at Hopkins, also confirmed the finding, saying that the otters' appearance "brought scientists as near to wild rejoicing as men of their profession are permitted."

In 1978 the range of the southern sea otter extended approximately from Santa Cruz to Pt. San Luis, just north of Avila, in San Luis Obispo County. Occasionally a half dozen or more will be seen north of Santa Cruz, and seasonally as many as 40 have visited the area of Manresa and Sunset State Beaches. Of a larger number that arrived at Soquel Point, only 40 or so (in 1978) seem to have established themselves on the north side of Monterey Bay. Stragglers have also been seen in the Santa Barbara area and as far south as Malibu. But at neither end of the range does the population seem to be making significant progress in the last few years.

There are several favorite viewing spots on the Monterey Peninsula, beginning with Wharf No. 2 in Monterey and "restaurant row" on Fisherman's Wharf. From the windows of almost any of the cafes on both wharves, the otters can be seen putting on a show. Competing with the seagulls for scraps of fish tossed from the incoming fishing boats, they seem to have developed a routine of marine acrobatics, to the delight of visitors. It has been suggested that the restaurants have further subsidized these entertaining beasts by tossing them other edible scraps, thereby making sure that they will be on hand to draw the customers.

The parking lot areas between the Tia Maria and Outrigger restaurants on Cannery Row are other good places to see them; also Otter Point on the Pacific Grove waterfront, immediately west of Lovers Point; Point Pinos; Point Joe and Bird Rock on the 17-Mile drive; also the Cypress Point pullout and Pescadero Point; Carmel Point and the various coves at Point Lobos State Reserve.

The beach at Alder Creek in southern Monterey County, the coastline immediately south of Piedras Blancas Point in San Luis Obispo County, and Montana de Oro State Park south of Morro Bay offer other possible grandstand seats, but trying to set a "best time" for otter appearances is always a gamble. In the Cannery Point and Sandhill Cove areas of Point Lobos, 4 pm has frequently been a good hour for viewing, but this cannot always be depended upon.

If all else fails, go to the Pacific Grove Museum of Natural

Off Cannery Row, in full view of their admirers on shore or at window seats in the restaurant in the background, two sea otters relax, warm themselves in the sun, and groom a little. The one on the right is in the typical position, on its back, with head, paws, and flippers out of the water, the otter's means of thermoregulation. The exposed parts release, conserve, or absorb heat in response to temperature of body, air, and water. The white-headed otter on the left appears to be rolling over. In doing this otters usually manage to keep both head and feet dry—quite a trick. (R.J. Western)

History, where there is an excellent mounted specimen in a glass case. This will give you an idea of the size of the creatures, and an indication of the handsomeness of their fur.

In the spring, when pupping takes place, mother otters and their pups can frequently be seen off Otter Point, Pacific Grove, through binoculars or spotting scopes, which are recommended for viewing at all times. For out in the giant kelp, *Macrocystis,* it is often difficult to distinguish the animals as the kelp moves under the tide and wave action. Another alga, *Nereocystis,* sometimes called "bull kelp," has large floats which bob on the surface and are frequently mistaken for otter heads, until brought

9

"They're in the kelp bed out there." Judson Vandevere, research biologist and investigator for the Friends of the Sea Otter, shows a young student where otters can be seen, from a ledge on the Big Sur coast.

Though most marine mammals are free-ranging and out of sight most of the time, the sea otter, especially in central California, occurs in kelp beds close to shore and rests, eats, grooms, and carries on courtship and mating at the surface, sometimes so near as to be readily observed even with the naked eye. In rough weather, however, when huge waves crashing on rocky shores pose a serious hazard, sea otters may raft at some distance from shore, even up to 3 miles away. (J.A. Mattison, Jr.)

into close focus through binoculars or scopes.

Looking like the original "old men of the sea," some of them may be seen holding their paws and flippers out of the water to regulate their body temperature, which at an even 100°F is slightly higher than a human's. Or they may occasionally come ashore to warm themselves. If they are feeling defensive or aggressive, they may do a good deal of growling or hissing, and may even bite one another when alarmed. Or they may embrace when frightened.

Divers' air bubbles sometimes alarm them. Their sensitive surveillance systems make them instinctly take evasive action, but being very curious, they are likely to return to make sure what

White head fur is seen mostly in males and in aging otters, but some females and some young of both sexes may have whitish heads. The body fur of adults is usually dark brown to black, but in older males the whole body may become grizzled with silvery hairs. (J.A. Mattison, Jr.)

is going on. The young often alert the adults to danger.

Persistence is one of their more outstanding characteristics, and they have been known to dive as often as 24 times to obtain one abalone. They have an easier time with sea urchins and an otter at Santa Cruz came up with a sea urchin every time in 12 successive dives. Turban snails on kelp require the shortest dives.

MOST YEARS an otter census is taken by the California Department of Fish and Game, aided by volunteer observers. A three-day exercise in 1976, combining aerial reconnaissance with 163 ground stations and utilizing 30 observers, counted 1,561 free-swimming otters between Pismo Beach on the south and Pigeon Point on the north. Pigeon Point is just above Año Nuevo

Distinctive profile of a rafting sea otter is easily recognized by the upright hind flippers, upraised head, and a body lying on its back and high in the water. (W. F. Bryan)

State Park in San Mateo County. Including an estimated 67 clinging pups, and allowing small variance for adults probably missed because underwater or otherwise hidden, the total population estimate was 1,856.

One otter was seen at Shell Beach, at the north end of Pismo Beach; 94 just north of Pecho Rock and 142 between Pecho Rock and Morro Bay. Far to the north, one otter was seen at Table Rock, north of Santa Cruz; one off Capitola and 46 between Seaside and Santa Cruz, with the northern front principally off the Salinas River and Manresa State Beach. The bulk of more than 1,500 was between Monterey Bay and Morro Bay.

THE FACT that less than 2,000 southern sea otters occupy this range, and that the historical range of the sea otter had shrunk by 90 percent, among other considerations, persuaded the U.S. Fish and Wildlife Service early in 1977, to declare this a "threatened" species. The Service added that "the remaining habitat and population is potentially jeopardized by oil spills and possibly other pollution and competition with man." The animal had already been protected under the Marine Mammal Protection Act of 1972 which contains a moratorium on killing. None may be handled without a scientific research permit.

12

The listing as "threatened" provides the additional protection of the "critical habitat" provisions of the Endangered Species Act, which will enable the Fish and Wildlife Service to determine the living space and other requirements of the sea otter, and will oblige all federal agencies to insure that their actions "do not impinge on the needs of the otter." However, no listing is permanent; for example, in 1978 the endangered species act was weakened and its future is uncertain. In addition, the state of Alaska has obtained a *waiver* of the moratorium that since 1972 has prohibited the killing of sea mammals in all American waters. As of January 1, 1979 there are annual kill quotas for various species of Alaskan sea mammals. The annual "take" for sea otters has been set at 3,000.

OCCASIONAL predation on otters by white sharks does occur in California, and there is also the possibility of attack by killer whales. In Alaska some sea otter pups are taken by bald eagles. However, for possibly 10,000 years or more, ever since the natives of the shorelines from which the otter could be hunted, set out to kill it for food and clothing, man has been the one predator whom the sea otter has constantly had to fear.

Otter rearing up, to examine its surroundings when startled. The protrusion of the hind flippers, as well as the head, makes it easy to distinguish a swimming sea otter from a seal or a sea lion. (J.A. Mattison, Jr.)

Otter eating, with rock on chest, is irresistible to any photographer, but a picture like this usually requires a boat, a calm day, and a steady hand on the camera button. (J. A. Mattison, Jr.)

A pop bottle as anvil is sometimes as handy as a rock (T. Hardy)

2

FLOATING ANVILS OF THE SEA

A TOUR BUS rounding Carmel Point stopped suddenly when its passengers began "oohing" and "ahing" at a scene in the water below. A group of otters had found an automobile hubcap and were tossing it back and forth in a game of water frisbee. Incredulous, the bus riders swarmed out onto the side of the road, accompanied by the driver, who said that he had never seen anything like it during a life of driving up and down the coast of Monterey County.

Camera shutters were clicking all over the place as the tourists tried to obtain pictorial proof of the event. Unfortunately the otters were less than cooperative and moved farther out into the bay, where the hubcap finally disappeared. Then the bus driver had his toughest job of the day, trying to persuade everyone to get back into the seats so that the tour could proceed.

Commenting on this episode, Jud Vandevere said that although he had seen it in print in a local newspaper, he thought frisbee tossing by otters was anatomically impossible, since they don't have thumbs and can't get that sort of grip onto anything similar to a frisbee. "But I've seen otters do all sorts of other things I wouldn't have believed possible," he concluded. Dr. Betty Davis, University of California zoologist, believes that there is nothing to prevent otters from tossing hubcaps, using both forepaws.

Otters are remarkably adept with their "hands," or forepaws, and have well-developed pads in the palms. While there has never been a second report, as far as this writer knows, of their taking up frisbee tossing as a game or choosing up sides for water polo, they have learned to use tools, such as rocks and pop bottles, to break shellfish loose from rocks and to crack them open before eating.

The small forepaws have sensitive pads and sharp claws. In clear and calm water, otters can see some food objects from the surface. But at night, and in turbid water, searching out food depends upon the sensitive whiskers and especially the forepaws, which "pad" the bottom and rock crevices. (R. Buchsbaum)

Nothing pleases an otter-watcher more than to see an otter dive for a rock or two and bring them to the surface, where the otter will float on its back and place the larger rock on its chest to serve as an anvil. The shellfish will then be held in a forepaw and cracked against the anvil, or if necessary, a second rock (or even a pop bottle) will be used as a hammer on the mussel, clam, or other food item. This trick of using tools is said to place the sea otter in a category with people, chimpanzees, certain solitary wasps *(Ammophila)*, Egyptian vultures, and Galapagos finches, the only other animals known to use tools habitually.

The otter's hindpaws, incidentally, are not as well padded. They are webbed and provide part of the mechanism for swimming, at which time the front paws are ordinarily held against the chest. The tail serves as a rudder.

"A floating anvil of the sea"—an otter with a rock on chest or belly. This one is resting between dives and swimming slowly by alternate strokes of the hind flippers and gentle vertical movements of the flattened tail, said to be used like a "sculling oar." Otters are the only sea mammals that move from one area to another at the surface and on their backs. Surface speed on the back may reach 1.75 miles per hour. More rapid swimming at the surface is done belly down. (R. Buchsbaum)

Divers have also observed otters taking huge rocks with them as ballast on deep dives to speed their descent. And if the rock is not too big, it may be used to knock an abalone, or a clump of mussels or barnacles loose from an underwater ledge. Heavy canine teeth then pry open the molluscs. Broad, crushing molars help in crushing the harder shells and getting at the meat.

When boaters began to toss flip-top cans overboard and these settled to the bottom, they became favorite hiding places for small octopuses. It didn't take the otters long to discover this and to tear open the cans with their canine teeth to obtain a meal.

Cracking a bivalve against a rock held on the chest—or sometimes against another clam—is a sea otter habit much enjoyed by otter-watchers. (J.A. Mattison, Jr.)

Breaking open a clam by pounding it on a rock is not always as easy as it is cracked up to be. One otter was seen to use 85 whacks to crack a mussel. Usually this job can be done with 35—the whole sequence, from first blow to final gulp, taking only about 45 seconds. (R. Buchsbaum)

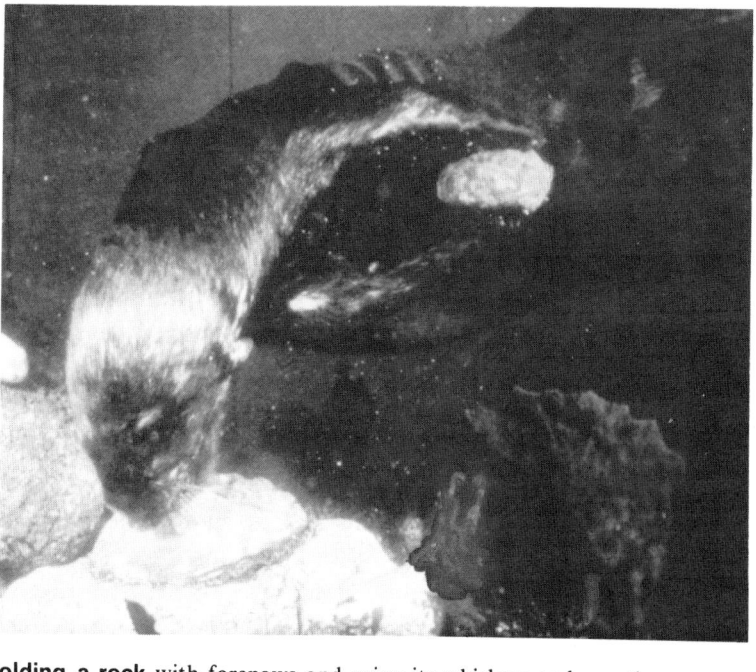

Holding a rock with forepaws and using its whiskers and mouth, an otter explores an abalone (Ron Church)

Using the rock as a tool the otter breaks the edge of the abalone's shell, helping to loosen the tight hold by which the abalone clings to the rocky bottom. (Ron Church)

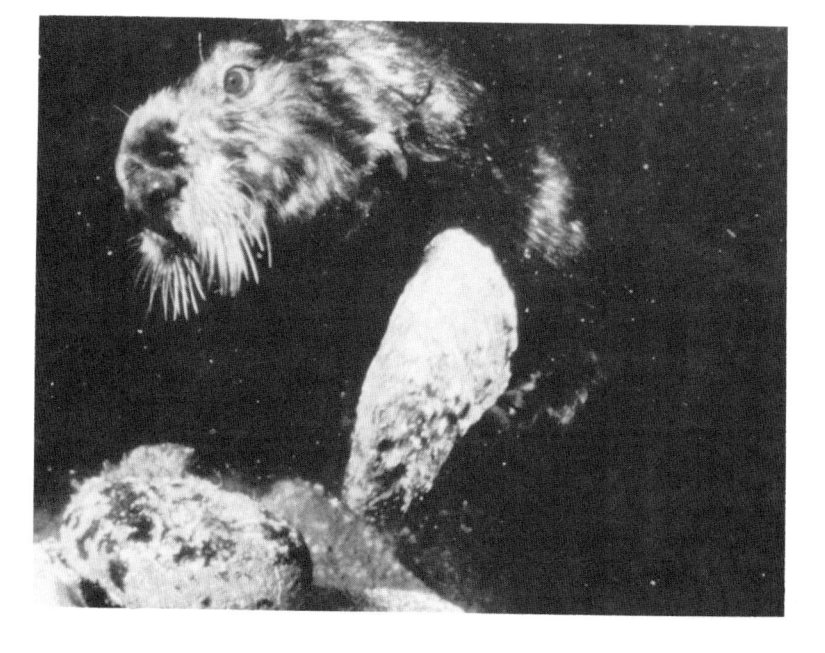

SOME YEARS AGO a female otter was captured off Alaska's Amchitka Island and kept for six years with constant care and attention at Seattle's Woodland Park Zoo, where she was named Susie. Susie became so attached to her pet rock, with which she broke clams, that she would not let it out of her sight. But when she began chipping the concrete edges of her tank with it, and pounding the drain and breaking it, the rock had to be removed. Susie's story was included in an article written for *National Geographic Magazine* by Karl Kenyon, who became an advisor to the U.S. Marine Mammal Commission after retiring from the U.S. Bureau of Sport Fisheries and Wildlife. Susie died about the age of seven, but during those years she provided scientific data which has keyed a great deal of research since.

Adult male sea otters in Seattle Zoo, Washington (8 July 1969). (V. B. Scheffer)

3

A SEA OTTER'S BUSY DAY AND NIGHT

ON A FOGGY MORNING a few years ago, I went out from the Monterey marina in a small cruiser belonging to the California Department of Fish and Game. Warden Warren Smith, a specialist in sea otters, who frequently lectured in public schools of Monterey County, had promised to take me to a spot offshore from Point Pinos, so that I could photograph a large "raft" or herd of sea otters, to illustrate a feature article I was writing for the *Monterey Peninsula Herald*.

When we were 100 yards or more from the kelp bed which the 30 or so otters considered home, a fellow warden of Smith's, who was at the wheel, cut the engine so that we could drift in noiselessly. It was still foggy, and in the gray light, with the boat swaying up and down, I was having difficulty focusing on the animals' heads. As soon as I had a sharp image on the groundglass, they disappeared. I kept shooting, but it seemed as if the heads bobbed up constantly between shots, rather than when I pressed the button. "They're laughing at you," said Warren Smith, who was laughing himself.

The prints, which turned out gray as the fog, almost proved it.

When Smith talked to schoolchildren, he took with him an otter pelt, from an adult animal found dead on the beach, to show how rich and thick the fur is, and why it was so prized during the 18th and 19th centuries by hunters who pursued the animal to near-extinction. It has a dense undercoat which most investigators believe traps tiny bubbles of air and serves as an insulating blanket against the cold of the ocean. However, Dr. Tom Williams suggests that the dense fur, with its natural oils, acts like a scuba diver's wet suit holding a layer of body-warmed water close to the skin. The fur must be constantly preened and cleaned to retain its effectiveness. In fact, whenever a sea otter isn't eating or sleeping, it seems to be grooming its fur. It is the only sea mammal which, because of its lack of a thick layer of body fat, must rely solely on its fur for retaining its body heat.

The fur of the sea otter is more dense than that of any other mammal. One sample of skin, from an adult male, that died at the Seattle Zoo, was estimated by Victor Scheffer to contain 650,160 hairs to the square inch (perhaps twice as dense as in the fur seal). The hairs are arranged in discrete bundles separated by minute areas of bare skin. Each bundle of hairs emerges through a single pore in the skin and consists of 60 to 80 underfur hairs and a single guard hair. The underfur hairs are extremely fine, roughly one-tenth as thick as the average hair of an adult human. Guard hairs of otters vary more, and are about 6 to 10 times thicker than the hairs of the underfur. The guard hairs serve as a protective shield, and each has a flattened, bladelike tip.

Sea otter hair lies very flat when wet, preventing the intrusion of cold water. This otter is finishing up a morning meal and lies relaxed, with the hind flippers at rest. (R. Buchsbaum)

Associated with the bundles of hairs are sweat glands, and also oil-secreting glands that help to make the fur water-repellent. When otters are experimentally soiled with crude oil, then cleaned with detergents, and finally replaced in the water and allowed to groom, they tend to sink and usually soon die. Allowing the cleaned otter to remain out of the water for several days until the hairs recover their natural oil produces better results.

The flattened tips of the guard hairs mesh together closely when in the water, and this together with the absence of any hair-raising muscles, allows the fur to lie very flat, presenting a surface that resists the penetration of cold water.

Molting is not as apparent in sea otters as it is in land mammals which molt conspicuously during warm months. Asian sea otters are said to have longer and denser fur in winter, and studies on Alaskan sea otters suggest that the animals do shed most in late spring and summer, least in winter. But both Alaskan and Californian sea otters show appreciable shedding in all months, and to the casual observer the pelage appears much the same in all seasons.

Though heat loss in water is at least 25 times faster than in air at the same temperature, the extraordinary fur of the sea otter cuts heat loss in water to only 20 percent more than heat loss in air. Nevertheless, the dependence on fur instead of blubber has serious drawbacks and is the central fact in the life of the sea otter. The special features of its physiology and habits, that make the animal unique in so many ways, are all directed toward helping the otter cope with the stress of cold.

Comparing the sea otter with its relative the river otter helps one to understand some of the adaptations of the sea otter to cold water—even though the river otter is also known for its hardiness in Canadian winters and for entering Pacific waters occasionally to dive and feed. The sea otter is larger in size, which helps in a cold environment, but its heart is smaller in proportion to body weight than that of the river otter; perhaps the greater buoyancy of salt water requires less effort. The sea otter liver is larger in proportion to body weight than that of the river otter—not surprising for an organ that must process and store the great quantities of energy-yielding substances required to support high heat loss. The kidney of a sea otter is more than twice as large, for the animal's size, as that of the river otter. Again, this could be expected in an animal with a very high metabolic rate, a diet of salty animals, and a habit of drinking salt water every day.

The lungs of the sea otter are exceptionally large—about 2.5 times the volume of the lungs of land mammals of comparable size. This adds to the buoyancy provided by the air-filled fur, and it permits the large store of oxygen needed during dives. The dives are rarely deeper than 120 feet, and usually no more than 40 feet deep when foraging for food.

Fully grown male sea otters in California average 58 pounds; and adult females about 41 pounds, as mentioned earlier. Of course, there are juvenile sea otters and these must be taken into account when estimating the total weight of the population and their food requirements.

In the water the energy needs of a resting sea otter are three times those of terrestrial animals of equal size. And to maintain its metabolic rate the sea otter must daily eat perhaps 25 percent of its body weight (estimates range from 20% to 37%). To do this the otters feed by night as well as by day, grooming before and after each feeding. Together, feeding and grooming occupy nearly half the 24-hour "day" of a sea otter.

There is no strict rhythmicity to the sea otter's day, as there is for animals that feed only in the light, or only at low tide, or must pursue prey that comes out only at particular hours of the day or night. The prey of southern sea otters is mostly sedentary or sessile, sitting quietly and ready to be picked off the rocks or kelp at any hour of the day or night that the otter feels hungry or too cold.

Thomas Loughlin, working near Monterey, tagged 24 animals with color-coded and numbered tags, and equipped some of these with radiotelemetry collars so that he could monitor their 24-

Otters feed alone and rarely allow other otters near them during feeding. Each has a preferred feeding site at some distance from the rafting area, and this usually avoids conflicts. The otter shown here was eating an abalone held in the forepaws. After finishing the fleshy part of the abalone, the otter held the empty shell out at arms length, then licked it until it shone like a mirror in the late afternoon sun. Then it repeated the examination and meticulous licking several times. (R. Buchsbaum)

hour activity patterns. He obtained records of the "active time" involved in feeding, grooming, play, or other goings-on, but not the small "comfort movements" that otters make while rafting. He found that otters may forage for food at any time and that they do much the same things by night as by day, and in the same places. The various behaviors occurred in large time-blocks. No feeding bout lasted less than an hour, and on average each took about 2.5 hours, day or night, males or females. Usually there were three feeding bouts: morning, late afternoon, and night. But there could be as many as five, with two during the night. Total feeding time occupied about one-third of the otter's day, but this amounts to almost three-fourths of its "active time." In a 24-hour period otters were active about half the time and rafting the other half. In the daytime they rested from late morning through early afternoon, the warmest part of the day.

Mother dives while the pup, unable to dive yet, watches and waits for her return. (R. Buchsbaum)

Dives lasted close to a minute, and the longest recorded dive a little over 4 minutes (considerably less than those of seals or whales). In the daytime, at least, otters came up with food items in about 75% of the 1500 dives recorded; but success and length of dive varied with type of food. Clams required the longest time, up to two minutes. Collecting *Cancer* crabs averaged about a minute. Kelp crabs and sea urchins required only about a 50-second dive. Abalones may take only a minute, but many dives may be required to loosen one from its tight hold on the rocks. Easiest of all were the turban snails; they could be snatched off kelp or off the bottom in 45 seconds but are not much of a mouthful; the otter must collect many of them to satisfy its hunger. Otters munching on sea stars are usually seen to bite off only the tips of the arms and to be sucking out the gonads in the angles between the arms, but most of the animal is then thrown back and often regenerates. At Monterey about 1% of the diet of otters is *Pisaster giganteus,* a subtidal sea star; and about half the individuals examined in that area have regenerated one or more arms.

Common food items of the sea otter diet. (R.W. Cooke III)

Fortunately, otters are opportunistic feeders, and 49 different items eaten by California sea otters have been recorded. In Alaska the records cite 72 items. Otters favor sea urchins, abalones, *Cancer* crabs, and clams—all high-calorie items that are worth the expenditure of energy to collect. When these are in short supply otters turn to snails, limpets, chitons, mussels, rock scallops, worms, and other less energy-efficient foods.

In California, sea otters do not eat fishes (perhaps because the fishes in these waters are too fast for them, or perhaps there is sufficient invertebrate food that is easier to obtain). Studies show that the feeding habits of sea otters promote the kelp forests that shelter and feed many fishes. The wide-ranging tastes of sea otters enable them to eat many animals that increase rapidly, while sparing those that are in short supply; and such feeding habits are important, perhaps critical, in maintaining a natural balance in the plant and animal communities of the intertidal areas and the kelp forests.

Heavy whiskers are important sense organs underwater, but when sea otters pop up to see what is going on around them, they are all eyes, ears, and smell. In daytime foraging, vision supplements the forepaws and whiskers in searching out food on the bottom. On land, smell may be more important than hearing as a warning sense. The animal has relatively small ear canals but large and complex nasal cavities. Otters on land may not react to a human intruder until the wind suddenly shifts in their direction. (J.A. Mattison, Jr.)

Swimming near the bottom, the otter maneuvers by stroking or paddling movements of the hind flippers and tail. This otter has just picked a large sea cucumber from the bottom and will surface at once. But if it should delay to pick up the two sea urchins seen on the bottom, at the left, it would store the cucumber in the large underarm skin fold. Otters appear to be right-handed; all those observed by Kenyon in Alaska used the right forepaw to place food items under the left underarm. (J.A. Mattison, Jr.)

Sea otter returning to surface with an urchin. (J.A. Mattison, Jr.)

Encounter underwater between two feeding otters usually results in the larger or more aggressive animal making off with the food of the other. These otters appear to be too distracted to take notice of the photographers and their bright lights. (J.A. Mattison, Jr.)

A gull swoops down on a not-too-wary, feeding sea otter ...

An otter finishing a clam. (Judy Campbell)

... **and makes off** with part of its shellfish meal. The gull turns its back on the not-too-anguished sea otter, which is seen to the right of the gull with paw to mouth, guarding what is left of its meal. (J.A. Mattison, Jr.)

Eating a large red urchin, with or without pounding on a rock, takes knowhow! After cracking the globular shell, the otter gets at the soft viscera within, often using a forepaw to ladle out the masses of eggs or sperms. Forepaw infections, from puncture wounds by spines, are common—perhaps more so in polluted bays. (J.A. Mattison, Jr.)

Crushing a clam with strong teeth and powerful jaw muscles, this big male uses his flattened and rounded molars to break the shell into small pieces. He will then remove the soft contents with canines and tongue. Even the canines have blunt tips, which become worn or broken when used to open hard shells. Otter teeth are adapted for crushing invertebrates with hard shells, not for tearing flesh. (R. Buchsbaum)

The otter may break the abalone shell while taking it from its attachment on the bottom. (Betty Randall)

A sea otter partaking of abalone steak au naturel. (J. A. Mattison, Jr.)

Wet fur, briefly shaken after the otter is freshly emerged, shows points formed by the sticking together of the wet tips of the guard hairs. The underfur is relatively dry. (R.J. Western)

GROOMING has second priority, after feeding, in the sea otter's day. As mentioned earlier, the animal depends for maintenance of a constant high body temperature on having meticulously groomed its air-filled fur that keeps the cold water away from its skin. Sea otters have short bouts of grooming just before feeding, in which they "warm up" as they prepare the fur for diving in the cold water. After each feeding there is a session (about 25 min.) of grooming. Each long bout follows a definite sequence, illustrated in the photos. There are also brief groomings during resting periods and after various kinds of activity. In all, grooming usually occupies at least 3 of the 24 hours.

Grooming after feeding begins, even while the otter is on its way back to the kelp bed, with repeated somersaults and rolls. Air thus trapped in the fur is rubbed in vigorously with the forepaws—first over the entire body and then especially into the back, nape, and base of the tail, areas with the densest fur and that remain longest in the water. The skin is loose and can be pushed around in order to get at these hard-to-reach areas. The early stages of grooming, when the otter is ruffling the fur, also help to dissipate excess body heat developed during strenuous feeding. Here the animal has squeezed water out of the fur and is licking the wet forepaws. (R.J. Western)

Partly groomed otter, wrapped in kelp, is working on the dense fur of the chest, face, and feet. Shaking the head is of some help. The paws are rubbed together, and so are the flippers; and both limbs and tail are thoroughly licked. Besides rubbing and licking the fur, the otter appears to blow air into it. The white scar on the nose is presumably the result of a mating enounter, in which the male holds onto the female by grasping her nose with his teeth. (R.J. Western)

Late stage of grooming is more leisurely. The otter licks its paws and chest, rubs the rear flippers together, and gently massages its face and jaw. Though grooming after feeding is more intensive than at other times, and follows a definite sequence that lasts about 25 minutes, there are briefer groomings at other times, especially just before diving. In all, an otter spends about 3 to 4 of the 24 hours grooming, mostly during the resting period from late morning to early afternoon. (J.A. Mattison, Jr.)

Thoroughly groomed otter, wrapped in *Macrocystis*, rests in a sun-warmed kelp bed, drying its upraised head and limbs. (John D. Mattison)

OTTER WATCHERS never tire of the spectacle of an otter furiously whacking a clam against a rock held on the chest; nor do they pass up a chance to see an otter munching on a sea urchin or a crab while at the same time nursing a large pup that appears to be as big as the mother as it floats out at right angles to her body. However, some serious observers yearn for "something more" and have taken their binoculars or telescopes to the shore to help with the otter census organized by the California Department of Fish and Game. Others have found that it adds interest and focus to their random observations if they record anything that seems novel, together with appropriate notes on location, time of day, and date. When made carefully, such records can contribute to what is known about sea otter distribution or habits. If they seem to be of sufficient interest or amusement they can be sent to *The Otter Raft* (at P.O. Box FF, Carmel, CA 93921) or brought to the office of the "Friends of the Sea Otter" in the Barnyard in Carmel Valley. When otters turn up at locations beyond their usual range, records of sightings that give otter numbers, location, and date, could be of interest to scientists at the Department of Fish and Game in Monterey.

TRYING TO LEARN something about how otters relate to each other is another matter. Each otter under observation has to be recognized as an individual, so the otters must be tagged. Moreover, a particular group of otters must be observed systematically and over a long period of time—almost always a job for professionals. The account that follows is based mostly on the 1975 to 1977 study by Thomas Loughlin on sea otters he tagged at Monterey Bay.

A raft of sea otters is not a brief or chance assemblage. Otters are gregarious, and a number of animals can share the same kelp bed with remarkably little friction. Fights are rare; the few observed by Loughlin usually occurred when a male approached another male enjoying the company of a female. Perhaps congeniality is made easier by segregation of the sexes, and rafts are mostly either male or female. Females with young pups tend to raft away from other females, but later rejoin a female raft.

According to Karl Kenyon, writing of Alaskan sea otters, independent juveniles tend to wander about and enter a raft of either sex though they are more likely to join a raft composed of members of their own sex. Adult males are more likely to intrude into female rafting areas than females are to enter male areas, but females moving about to feed do cross male preserves. Either situation provides opportunities for males to determine whether a female is in estrus and to make himself available, if not always acceptable. Courting and mating in otters can take place at any season of the year.

In California, rafts of two to six are most common and few exceed 16; one large raft off Hopkins Marine Station in 1970 included 140 otters, and a raft of 170 has been observed farther south. The rafting area of a sea otter, usually in a kelp bed, is the area to which the animal consistently returns, over many weeks or months, mostly to rest and to groom. Juveniles play actively there and grown-ups intent on something more serious may court and mate there. As with humans, older animals seem to be more settled, returning each time to the same resting site within a rafting area. Even young animals are reasonably faithful to a resting site within an area of roughly 300-600 square feet.

An otter feeds mostly at some distance from its rafting area and usually in or around a kelp forest, though sometimes in an open area with sandy bottom. An individual tends to forage in the same preferred feeding site over long periods; one otter tagged by Loughlin fed in the same area, just west of Hopkins Marine Station, for 18 months. Of course, otters do venture occasionally into places other than their preferred sites, though this involves some risk of an encounter with a bigger or nastier neighbor and the loss of some of the food collected. After feeding, females without pups swim back to their preferred rafting site, but those with pups tend to delay their return for 12 to 48 hours, continuing to rest and feed in the foraging area.

A raft of sea otters, is, for the most part, either a male or a female aggregation. (J.A. Mattison, Jr.)

Conserving body heat by holding head and limbs out of the cold water, one of these relaxed otters exposes the plastic identification tags placed on the flippers by investigators. The numbers on the tags can be read with the aid of binoculars and help to keep track of the movements, the home range, and some of the daytime habits of individual otters. (R. Buchsbaum)

The rafting area of an otter, together with the area in which it forages and feeds, is called its *home range,* and this usually consists of a narrow strip extending along the coast between the shoreline and the seaward edge of a kelp bed. As otters feed mostly on the bottom, a home range is a three-dimensional space; but topography varies, and it is easier to measure only the extent of the range at the sea surface. The home range of a California male sea otter is about 100 acres, and that of a female almost twice that area, averaging close to 200 acres.

Loughlin defines a territorial male as one that rests and forages in an exclusive home range or *territory,* in which he does not allow any other male to raft. Such a territory is always adjacent to a female raft, and it occupies only about two-thirds of the surface area of the home range of a nonterritorial male (one that rafts with other males). The territorial male makes brief visits to the adjoining female raft, seeking females in estrus. If he finds one, he may mate with her in the female rafting area. Or he may lure her, or drag her, to his own rafting site.

WHEN TWO MALES get sufficiently aroused to fight, they approach each other to within two body lengths and rise vertically out of the water high enough to expose about half the chest. They stare at each other, with teeth bared and shoulders hunched; and after a few seconds one lunges at the other, aiming for a bite at face or neck. The paws are used to ward off blows or to push the opponent around. The animals dive repeatedly, and most of the fight takes place under the surface. Fights may last only a few seconds, but if they continue for minutes they can be bloody. When one animal flees, the fight is over. The winner does not follow, nor does he try to continue the conflict by driving the loser from the general area. Both otters then groom vigorously, and in doing so probably cool off in both the psychological and physical sense.

In the only fight observed by Loughlin in which one of the fighting males was tagged and therefore distinguishable, the winner was a resident male who had been foraging with a female companion. While the resident male was under water, the interloper left his own territory and made his way directly toward the female, jerked his head in the direction of her genital area, and then came up under the female, wrapped his forelegs around her chest, and clasped her by the armpits as he tried to drag her to his territory. The surfacing male-in-charge did not take kindly to this, and after he had driven off the intruder was still in possession of both his territory and his companion.

As fighting is rare, territorial males apparently maintain their territories by more subtle means. Typically, they swim the outline of their territory, and perhaps the threat of imminent attack is sufficient to deter most wanderers. A female may raft in a territory, presumably under the surveillance of the resident male, and female home ranges are more likely than male ones to overlap a territory. Neither females nor males, as they come and go through a territory on their way to feed, are likely to be molested. But if they should be so indiscreet as to delay too long, they risk an aggressive encounter and loss of some food they may be carrying.

KEEPING THINGS GOING smoothly among otters probably involves several kinds of communication, not all of which are necessarily perceived by human observers. Most conspicuous are the vocal signals, such as the cries of pups in distress or separated from their mothers, even temporarily, as by a rock. From birth through the large juvenile stage, pups open their mouths wide to emit sharp "waah waah" cries that continue until reunion with the mother. For her part, a mother who has become separated from her pup may utter open-mouthed screams that can be heard, according to Kenyon, for up to one-half mile. Aside from concerned mothers, screaming in the adult is a sign of extreme physical distress, sometimes indicating the near approach of death in captive otters. They do not scream when being captured, but they may emit short explosive hisses or high-pitched whistles. When attempting to escape from a net they may snarl or utter deep-throated growls.

Satisfaction is also expressed vocally. The cooing of females, according to Kenyon, issues from the throat as a steady or intermittent "ku-ku-ku" that has been heard by human observers as much as 100 feet away. Females coo when especially pleased with food, when grooming, when fondling their pups, and before and after mating. Signs of satisfaction in the male, uttered while eating when very hungry, are described less kindly by human auditors as soft grunts. Otters also cough, sneeze, and yawn, like the rest of us, and we can only imagine what their otter friends make of all this.

A FORM of otter communication that escapes the casual observer could become an interesting challenge to sharp-eyed watchers once it has been brought to their attention. Loughlin has named it the "head jerk" and points out that "sea otters that are either leaving or entering a raft usually approach each individual in the raft or those directly in their path, and interact with these animals ...." The otter that makes the approach pushes its large and sensitive nose into the fur of the recipient, usually in the genital area but sometimes nearer to abdomen or chest, and moves the head sharply from the midline to one side in a sequence of at least two or three jerks—sometimes up to ten or more. If the jerking becomes intense, and lasts up to 30 seconds, the human observer presumes that a male has found an estrous female.

Head jerking is mostly a brief ritualized behavior, signalling friendly intent, as we judge from the fact that the recipient usually remains passive, as humans often do when they receive a brief friendly nod. Sometimes, however, the recipient rolls away or snaps back, and the human observer is left to consider whether the rebuffed otter has merely interrupted a nap, is too aggressive in manner, or is a male who has made advances to an unreceptive female. The information that is offered or elicited in head jerking could communicate age, social status, sex, and reproductive state, besides intent.

If an otter raft is not a completely "peaceable kingdom," at least head jerking and other forms of communication keep overt conflict to a minimum, saving a lot of fuss and fur. In cold seas, life for a warm-blooded animal without blubber is a continuing energy crisis. Good behavior, as they say, is its own reward; it conserves energy for the really important business of survival.

Close association of mother and pup for as long as eight months would seem to provide ample opportunity for learned behavior. Here a pup watches its mother groom a hard-to-reach area of fur. Distinguishing learned from inherited behavior patterns in mammals is difficult even with controlled experiments in the laboratory. However, much about the facts of behavior can be learned by careful observation of animals in the wild. (R. Buchsbaum)

4

SEA OTTER PUPS

IN 1977 there were three Alaskan otters flourishing in captivity in Tacoma and five California sea otters at Sea World, San Diego, including one pup, *Rosie,* rescued from high seas at Garrapata Beach south of Carmel. Rosie had been washed ashore and was spotted on the beach by a woman who called the nearby Department of Fish and Game mariculture laboratory. Attempts were made to return the pup to the nearshore kelp bed, where it might have been reunited with its mother, but rough water made the reunion impossible and the experiment was abandoned.

Instead, Rosie was turned over to Ron Jameson, a U.S. Fish and Wildlife researcher making observations on the California sea otter population, and became part of the Jameson household for a few days pending transfer to Sea World. To quote from Dr. Betty S. Davis, executive secretary of the Friends of the Sea Otter, writing in the organization's publication, *The Otter Raft:*

"Rosie weighed around six pounds, was less than a month old, lacked the tawny coat of older pups, couldn't swim or dive, and lost several baby teeth while at the Jamesons' (possibly in Ron's arm). She was housed there in a cardboard box on clean, frequently changed towels and was fed on demand every four or five hours during the day, but slept during the night. Rosie was docile and delightful when well fed, but nippy and noisy when hungry. She accepted a formula developed by Borden Milk Co. for river otters, but much preferred squid.

"The daily routine started at 5:30 a.m. when Rosie was cleaned up, fed, and then placed in a bathtub of water to float and roll around; this usually stimulated defecation, and a bath after eating became a must.

Rosie, an orphaned pup, at 3½ months. Despite the combined efforts of the staff at Sea World, and Rosie's own grooming of areas she could reach by herself, Rosie's fur is visibly matted. A young sea otter apparently requires the constant grooming of the mother and the strong circulation of water in the ocean. The whiskers of captive animals grow longer than in wild otters, who wear them down as they forage on rocky bottoms. (Sea World, San Diego)

"When she signaled that she was tired of the water, Rosie was removed, thoroughly dried, and intensively groomed for over an hour by Ron, who rubbed her fur vigorously and blew air into it as mother otters do. Occasionally Rosie would attempt to groom herself but though she could bend as far as her hind flippers, she could not reach her back or certain other areas.

"When allowed to romp on the living room floor, much to the joy of young Steve and Robin, Rosie used every type of locomotion observed in otters—she humped and hopped along, dragged her hind flippers, walked with alternate steps in river otter fashion, and almost galloped.

"Six days after rescue, Rosie was taken in a box, on clean dry towels, to Sea World in a Fish and Game plane with Dr. Tom Williams, a veterinarian who is a member of the Friends advisory committee and who has a DFG permit to care for otters in distress, and Ron Jameson in attendance. When she whistled shrilly from heat stress en route, they cooled her off with water.

"At Sea World Rosie occupies a $9' \times 3'$ tank of water separated from the three adults now there. She can get in and out of the water by herself, is fed shrimps and clams, and is gaining weight. She is groomed by attendants routinely since this needed cleanliness appears to be a key to success for husbandry of young otters. Rosie was in great shape on delivery and it will be a triumph if she continues to thrive."

Raising otter pups to adulthood in captivity, however, is a tricky business. Despite all the expertise and constant care at Sea World, San Diego, Rosie lived only about seven months.

A DOZEN YEARS earlier, I had gone to the Pacific Grove Museum of Natural History to see another pup which had been similarly rescued after being stranded on the beach. It was a cute and friendly animal which appeared in good health, was given every kind of attention which seemed necessary, but died en route to San Diego by car. Warren Smith and his wife Margaret, who made the trip for the Department of Fish and Game, said later that they felt too much time was lost by automobile. Thus later trips, as with Rosie, were made by plane. But even after safe arrival, there is no guarantee that a pup will adapt completely to a Sea World environment, which cannot fully duplicate the ocean. An important factor may be that pups need lots of grooming and are not always adept enough to handle this alone.

At Tacoma's Point Defiance Aquarium, where several otter pups have been born in captivity, none has lived longer than 55 days although completely healthy at the outset. Research on the baffling causes of this has been continuous. The father is Gus, a 16-year-old male taken there by Karl Kenyon in 1965. Two females half that age have been there since 1969. At first it was thought that the "otterarium" was too exposed to public view, and that visitors startled the animals by suddenly appearing close to them. So a buffer zone was established that kept the public 15 feet away from windows of a large pool. Windows of a smaller pool were kept covered, with a passage between the pools left open. The otters, however, spent 90 percent of their time in the large pool where they could watch the public. Tacoma has been considering a separate tank for females with pups, as they often isolate themselves in the wild. Aquariums in Seattle and Vancouver, B.C., also with otters on view, have been reported studying the progress of Tacoma's experiments.

THERE HAVE BEEN several successful attempts to reunite pups with their mothers after the pups have been accidentally swept up onto the beach. The technique involves taking the pup out through the surf and floating it in the offshore kelp beds, where its cries usually attract its mother quite rapidly.

AN OTTER'S LIFE SPAN is thought to be between 15 and 20 years, and females become sexually mature at about four years of age. In courtship, otters nuzzle, with male and female sometimes swimming together for an hour at a time. A mating pair often stays together for three or four days, and copulation takes place in the sea. Sea otters are generally believed to give birth to one pup in two years. Vandevere has reported that a California female (tagged in August 1976 by Loughlin) had a pup in January 1977 and again in February 1978, only five months after she had weaned her dependent pup. He hopes to follow this apparently prolific female in 1979 and to make observations of other tagged females. So far as is known, California sea otters give birth in the sea. (In Alaska otters usually come ashore to give birth.)

Pupping in California takes place between December and March, reaching its peak in February. For about 8 months (in some cases less) the pup is dependent on its mother, and the females with their pups tend to raft together. So the observer with binoculars or scope is likely to see a variety of activity, and the interplay between mothers and pups is one of the most re-

"I've had enough of this swimming lesson," the three-week-old pup seems to be saying. The nearly helpless pup, lifted off the mother's chest and placed in the water, swims belly down, paddling with all four feet and crying out at intervals. Swimming on the back has to be learned and develops slowly. (R.B.)

warding experiences for the otter-watcher.

Pups have to learn to both swim and dive. At first, their fluffy bodies can do little more than float, but they soon begin to paddle alongside their mothers. First attempts to get their heads and/or tails under water may result in their bobbing up in a direction opposite to that which they had intended, but by the time they have attained medium size they can usually swim either on their backs or stomachs. Then they paddle along with head submerged to see what their mothers are doing. This is often preliminary to attempting a dive themselves.

Similarly the pups must learn to eat and to acquire solid food. Jud Vandevere tells of spending nine days with assistants watching one otter mother from dawn to dusk to record her feeding routine with her very young pup. To start it nursing, she would lift it from her chest and turn it around so that its head was close to the two nipples on her lower abdomen. After it had nursed, she turned it end for end and cleaned its face. When she herself fed, she again lifted the pup from her chest and floated it on the water while she made two short dives for crabs. Most of her days were spent licking and grooming the baby and of course herself.

Nursing pup lies on its relaxed mother as it sucks milk from one of the two nipples near the lower end of her abdomen. (Betty Davis)

Meanwhile a second mother was trying to interest a slightly older offspring in eating a crab by placing a small piece on the pup's chest. When the pup ignored the crab, the mother took it and consumed it. The next day, at the same place, the same mother repeated the experiment. This time her pup took the offering in its forepaws and tried tasting a small morsel. Presumably in another day or two, crab was on the pup's menu. And the same routine was doubtless followed by the other mother and pup.

Mother otters meticulously groom their pups, remove food particles from their fur and blow air into it to keep them clean and buoyant. Soon, instead of the mother's swimming under the floating youngster to place it on her chest while sculling along on her back, the pup will be able to climb on and off, nurse, fall

A floating pup, too young and buoyant to dive, and riding high in the water, awaits its mother's return from an underwater foraging expedition. In rougher water the fluffy pup bobs up and down like a floating cork. (R. Buchsbaum)

As the mother resurfaces, the pup utters a shrill "yip," rolls over, and starts to paddle with all fours in her direction. (R. Buchsbaum)

"Hey, Mom, wait a minute!" Pup travels faster as mother is about to sink her teeth into the abalone she has brought up. Nipples are visible on the lower part of her abdomen, but the pup is looking for something else. (R. Buchsbaum)

The abalone has been completely removed from its shell, now resting on the mother's chest, as the pup circles her, begging for a bite. (R. Buchsbaum)

When no morsel is immediately forthcoming, the pup clambers aboard its mother's floating body. (R. Buchsbaum)

"There's no point in being polite." The pup sinks its teeth into the delicious shellfish, while mother offers no real resistance. (R. Buchsbaum)

And having allowed her offspring to take a large chunk of the abalone, mother heads for the depths once more, to find another course for herself. (R. Buchsbaum)

asleep, change directions, or get into playful bouts with other pups. Ordinarily the adults will put up with quite a lot of boisterousness and tumbling about, but if the pups become too exuberant, especially when their mothers are trying to sleep, they will be dumped into the water and told to mind their manners.

Older pups, says Betty Davis, may occasionally purloin their mother's food and even her rock tool, "but eventually mother-pup food interactions evolve into a calm sharing of choice items.

"Stealing of food and tools continues on into adulthood but appears to be taken for granted by these sociable animals. Medium-sized and large pups may often be seen pounding their chests during feeding and grooming activities, perhaps copying their mothers, but only larger pups have been seen using a rock tool."

At the Coast Guard pier in Monterey, Betty Davis saw an otter mother and pup heading for Presidio Curve, where they hauled out on a nearshore rock, and the mother went to sleep. When Betty went to an overhanging embankment to investigate, the pup put its feet on the mother's head to wake her up and call her attention to Betty standing above. The pair then returned to the water where the pup, superbuoyant, tried to dive but couldn't, "just like a little balloon with head and feet submerged," said Betty, who returned to the area several times to see if the pair was still on hand. A couple of weeks later the pup had learned to dive.

Similar antics have delighted countless onlookers who have scrutinized the kelp beds at Point Lobos State Reserve and in Carmel Bay and the offshore "water beds" at Pacific Grove, all of them prime sites for otter nurseries. Increasing numbers of scientific researchers, students, teachers, and just everyday tourists have gathered to make their observations and add to the fund of knowledge about this enchanting creature with the inquisitive, bewhiskered face and furry body.

Grooming of young pup is done mostly by the mother. Immediately after its birth she may groom the pup continuously for nearly four hours, and then place it in position for nursing. Later she spends about 20 percent of daylight hours grooming her pup, working at it in periods of about 50 minutes each, with the majority of her efforts directed at the hind quarters where self-fouling occurs. (R. Buchsbaum)

Young pup in early attempt to groom itself, rests securely on the mother's belly as she heads back to the safety of a kelp bed after a bout of feeding. Such small pups may spend about ten percent of the time (recorded by human observers) in grooming themselves. Large pups groom 75 percent of observed time, but they still depend on their mothers for hard-to-reach places. (R. Buchsbaum)

Large nursing pup, floating on the water at an angle to the mother's body as she goes about eating her meal. Younger pups usually lie on the mother's body as they nurse. (R. Buchsbaum)

A mother cradles a sizeable pup in her arms. Pups stay close to their mothers less than a year. A tagged mother and her pup stayed together for eight months and were followed by Judson Vandevere. However, if the mother comes into estrus and attracts a male, she and the male will join forces to drive the pup away before they mate. (J. A. Mattison, Jr.)

5

THE HUNT FOR FURS

BY the late 17th century, sea otters were being hunted for their furs along the Kurile Island chain and the outer coast of the Kamchatka Peninsula. The Japanese were also hunting the animals north of Hokkaido. At the Russian and Chinese courts, and among the Japanese feudal families, sea otter fur was considered unsurpassed.

Otter, in fact, became the royal fur of China. Mandarins wore otter-skin robes. Their ladies wore otter capes, belts and sashes, hats and mittens, and used the fur for trimming on their silk gowns.

The most valued pelts were brownish-black in color, lustrous with silvery overhairs. Not even sable was thought comparable to the fine, soft, silky, shimmering otter, with its dense underfur and longer, slightly coarser overhairs.

If you have ever run your fingers through the fur of a sea otter pelt, you know that it gives a sensuous delight which is difficult if not impossible to match.

IN 1725 Czar Peter the Great appointed Vitus Bering, a Dane with a distinguished record in the Russian Navy, to head an expedition to determine if a land passage existed between Asia and North America. Five weeks later the Czar died. Bering continued with the assignment, explored the strait which now bears his name, but had to report on his return to the court of Catherine the Great that he had failed to reach the American coast. In 1740-41, during a second voyage, he discovered the Aleutian Islands and the Alaskan mainland, claiming them both for Russia. But in 1741, homeward bound for Siberia, he was stranded on what is now Bering Island, where he and some 30 other members of the expedition died of scurvy and other illnesses.

One of those to survive was German scientist Georg Wilhelm Steller, who, with other hunters, clubbed to death four sea otters in order to make a stew. Two accompanying cargo ships had been lost in a collision, provisions were reduced to starvation level, and the Russians, though they knew the value of the otter pelts, were then interested in the animals only as food. Later, the butchering of an immense sea cow (a species that was said to reach 30 feet and weigh 4 tons) and that was to be named for Steller, provided ample meat.

After a new and smaller ship had been built from the wreckage of the *St. Peter,* Bering's vessel, the remaining crewmen sailed it to Siberia, where Steller died, unable to capitalize on his share of 900 otter skins which had eventually been collected, and which sold for the equivalent of $30,000. He had made a study of the northern sea otter, so far as his personal observations on Bering Island permitted, and this was to remain a valued reference work. But the Russians were far more interested in the commercial possibilities of a new source of otter pelts—the fur that more than matched sable or ermine. Besides, land furs were getting increasingly hard to find; land fur-bearers had been too ruthlessly hunted for decades. Bering's shipwreck had suddenly revealed the otter and fur seal resources of the North Pacific.

According to William R. Hunt in *Arctic Passage,* "Russian traders swiftly responded to the possibilities of reaping fabulous wealth from the Bering Sea and organized expeditions to set out for the newly discovered islands."

It was 1783, however, before any base was established in Alaska. Then a Siberian merchant, Grigory Shelikhov, set up headquarters on Kodiak Island for hunting sea otters, seals, and foxes. By 1790 he was envisioning an expansion southward, even to California. Five years later, Shelikhov died, but his company became the nucleus of the Russian-American Company, granted a charter by Czar Paul I in 1799, and monopoly of all American operations.

The company's first manager was Alexander Baranov, who moved his headquarters to Sitka (called *Novo-Arkhangelsk* by the Russians) in 1804. The *promyshlenniki,* or "fur traders," had meanwhile been moving eastward, island by island along the Aleutians, and were trying to persuade the native Aleut hunters to accompany them.

The Aleuts used kayaks, called *baidarkas* by the Russians. The frames of these kayaks were made of thin strips of wood or whalebone, fastened together with whale or sea lion sinews. They were from 12 to 20 feet long, about 20 to 24 inches wide, and about 20 inches deep. Seal or sea lion skin was stretched over the entire frame, top and bottom, with every seam carefully sewed and the outer surface smeared with whale oil to make it waterproof.

From one to three openings were left in the top—usually two—giving just enough space for a man to kneel or sit and wield a double-bladed paddle. Each hunter wore a skin suit and fastened the lower edge of his jacket to a ring around the opening, thus keeping the craft from shipping water. In smooth seas these baidarkas could make 10 miles an hour with ease.

The weapon was a sort of primitive javelin with an arrowhead or bone-tipped dart at the end, loosely fitted into the shaft and joined to it by a long line of whale sinew.

The javelin was thrown from a wooden sling. When it scored a hit, the arrowhead lodged in the otter and was pulled loose from the shaft, which, as it was dragged through the water, retarded the diving animal greatly. The line could then be used to haul in the victim.

When a "raft" or herd of otters was sighted, the system called for from five to 20 baidarkas to try to encircle them, forcing them to dive repeatedly in the attempt to escape. When exhausted, they had to remain on the surface, an easy prey. (The average diving time for a feeding Alaskan adult male is 1.5 minutes; for a female, 1 minute. The period is shorter in California, usually from 30 to 60 seconds. The longest recorded escape dive was 4.25 minutes.)

Cruder hunting methods were used by the Pacific coast Indians, according to Adele Ogden in *The California Sea Otter Trade, 1784-1848.* They spread nets and snares on the kelp beds, then caught a sea otter pup and tied a cord to its foot. A pull on the cord caused it to cry out. When the mother responded and rushed to the rescue, she would be caught in the net and clubbed.

The otters, which had been quite tame when the Aleuts first arrived, allowing a baidarka or other boat to approach fairly close before diving, soon learned caution and developed many tricks to escape the hunters.

WHILE the Russians were moving southward, partly in search of a base where they could raise fruit and vegetables to feed their hunters and the men at Sitka—bringing supplies from Siberia was difficult and often impossible—the Spaniards in Alta and Baja California were just beginning to learn the value of the sea otter pelts. On a trip to Cerros Island off the west coast of Lower California in 1733, Fr. Sigismund Taraval had observed otters. Seamen killed 20 of them with sticks and the priest sent the skins to Mexico City. From about 1775 on, Spanish missionaries, soldiers, and seamen bartered beads, old clothes, and knives with the natives, in exchange for otter pelts. In 1783 the *Princesa,* a galleon on the Acapulco-Manila run, carried between 700 and 800 skins to the Orient.

IN 1776 Capt. James Cook, on a voyage of exploration for England, sailed up the northwest coast of America, where his sailors obtained skins for almost nothing, later selling them for fantastic prices in the Orient.

John Ledyard, an American on the Cook expedition, urged investors in the United States to look into this promising new business. When an account of the Cook voyage was published in 1784, corroborating Ledyard's statements, ships from the eastern U.S:, England, France, and Portugal set out for the Pacific Coast, and Spain prepared to enter the sea otter trade on an organized basis, hoping to keep out the foreign intruders.

At Monterey and Carmel, soldiers and mission padres traded with the Indians for furs. Though the Costanoan and Esselen tribes had not developed a hunting technique to equal that of the Northwest Indians, the number of sea otter bones found in the middens of excavated villages along the Central California coast, attests to the ability of these natives to acquire the pelts for their own use, hundreds of years before otter skins were shipped to the Orient via the Manila galleons.

In September 1784, according to Adele Ogden's research, the viceroy of New Spain, Vicente Vasadre y Vega, proposed a plan whereby vessels sent to California with supplies, should return to Acapulco with otter skins which would be taken to China and traded there for mercury, needed in mining gold.

In January 1787, Viceroy Bernardo de Galvez ordered this plan put into effect, the King of Spain having approved it. Vasadre was given a virtual monopoly of the sea otter trade. Gov. Pedro Fages in Monterey and Fr. Fermin Francisco de Lasuen at Carmel, were asked for their cooperation. In three months Vasadre visited nine missions, four presidios, and two pueblos, then in November left San Diego for San Blas with 1,060 skins, collected primarily from the missions at Carmel, San Antonio, San Luis Obispo, Santa Barbara, Ventura, and San Diego. Small wonder that he suggested exclusive mission control of the sea otter trade.

In Baja California, Missions San Vicente, Santo Domingo, Rosario, San Fernando, and San Francisco de Borja were added to the plan, which the padres enthusiastically approved as a measure to benefit the neophytes. A special supply of trading goods was sent to Monterey from Mexico City, to aid in barter.

Then in June 1787, the military, always at odds with the missions, somehow maneuvered into the act. New orders were issued, sending trade goods to the presidios for distribution. Soldiers were to be allowed to barter for skins.

In Manila, meanwhile, Vasadre was in trouble with the Philippine Company and Spanish government officials. This company had enjoyed a monopoly in bringing mercury from China. Vasadre was instructed to deal through the company and its agents in Canton. He refused, packed up, turned over his business to factors, and left for Spain. Between 1786 and 1790, however, a total of 9,729 otter skins had been sent to Manila. Vasadre had opened up the Spanish trade.

SOON thereafter, English merchantmen began appearing in California ports, to the alarm of the Spanish authorities. Viceroy Revilla Gigedo proposed Spanish explorations between San Francisco and what is now British Columbia to prevent foreigners from trading in otter skins, but this proposal was never carried out.

The first New Englander arrived off the Central California coast late in October 1796. He was Capt. Ebenezer Dorr, who anchored his Boston vessel, the *Otter,* opposite Carmel Mission. He was taking 1,000 skins, picked up on the northwest coast, to China by way of the Sandwich (Hawaiian) Islands, and had stopped for meat and water. Gov. Diego de Borica welcomed him, extended the hospitality of the port of Monterey, served him hot chocolate, and let him trade for eight cows, 1,000 pounds of meal, rice, beans, butter, tallow, and vegetables.

In August 1798, the firm of James and Thomas H. Perkins of Boston instructed James Rowan, captain of the *Eliza,* to go from the northwest to "Mont Rea" and then proceed to China. Rowan arrived at San Francisco in the spring of 1799, hoping to pick up enough otter skins to complete his cargo, and telling Spanish authorities that he needed wood and water. Gov. Borica, suspecting that skins might be smuggled aboard to circumvent the Spanish law of no trade with foreigners, only permitted Rowan to buy a few supplies, then ordered him out.

BY THE CLOSE of the 18th century, vessels were swarming into the North Pacific, most of them Yankee traders. When they put in at Spanish ports, it was with the excuse that they needed bread or other supplies, or had sprung a leak and needed repairs—

anything to permit them to stay long enough to deal with the *contrabandistas.* Spain attempted to tighten its restrictions on the traffic in otter skins, but its enforcement lacked manpower. The Yankee ships, avoiding the principal harbors, became bolder. The year 1803 showed a peak in contraband activity.

Resting sea otter wrapped in kelp is vulnerable. (J. A. Mattison, Jr.)

6

PIRATES AND PILLAGERS

L OGS AND LEDGERS of ships sailing along the northern
Pacific coast in the early years of the 19th century showed
that there were very few sea otters between the Strait of Juan de
Fuca and the northern California coast. San Francisco Bay
abounded in them, however, and there were considerable numbers at Bodega Bay, which was one of the reasons for the Russians establishing their southernmost base there in 1809, though
in 1812 they moved to Fort Ross as a better place for agricultural
pursuits.

Between San Francisco and Monterey, otter colonies were
noted at Pillar Point on Half Moon Bay, at Point Año Nuevo,
and at Santa Cruz Point and Bay. The records showed large
numbers in the kelp off Point Sur, along the coast around
Cooper's Point, at San Simeon, along the coastline opposite San
Luis Obispo, and at Point Conception. There were a few around
Santa Barbara, San Pedro, and San Juan Capistrano.

The largest otter rafts in the south were not off the mainland,
but in the kelp beds off the Santa Barbara Channel Islands, with
smaller numbers at Santa Catalina and San Clemente islands.

Sebastian Vizcaino, who sailed north from Mexico in 1602 in
search of pearl fisheries and was the first white man to come
ashore at Monterey, wrote of having seen Indians dressed in sea
otter skins on the Santa Barbara Channel Islands. Later
explorers described long capes of otter pelts, highly prized by the
aboriginal population of California, and other articles of
clothing, plus bed covers and arrow quivers made of sea otter
skins.

In Lower California, sea otters were plentiful at Todos Santos
Bay and Island, at the Santo Tomas anchorage, Colnett Bay, San

Quintin and Rosario bays, San Geronimo Island, Santa Rosalia and Sebastian Vizcaino bays, and Natividad, Cedros, and San Benito islands. Guadalupe Island, some distance to the west, also had a number of the animals. The southernmost hunting place mentioned was Morro Hermoso.

IN 1803 Capt. Joseph O'Cain, a New Englander, sailed to Kodiak Island, where he told Gov. Baranov of recently discovered islands off the Baja California coast abounding in sea otters. If Baranov would supply the Aleut hunters and the baidarkas, he would supply his ship, the *O'Cain,* he said, and split the proceeds 50-50. A contract was signed forthwith.

In June of the following year he returned and turned over half of 1,100 pelts which the Aleuts had taken. He also had 700 additional pelts which he had purchased from Spanish officials and missionaries. He had hunted off Guadalupe, Natividad, Cedros, and Redondo islands, had put in at San Diego on the return voyage with a plea for supplies, but had been turned down by port authorities who were strictly observing the law of no trade with foreigners. Nevertheless there were Spaniards who saw no reason for not selling skins to him.

The next year he arrived in Sitka with 3,000 prime skins plus the pelts of 1,264 yearlings and 549 pups.

In 1806 three more Boston ships signed similar contracts with the Russians and had similar problems with the Spaniards, though Capt. George Washington Eayrs of the *Mercury* had great success trading dishes, knives, saws, farm implements, and cloth to Spanish officials and padres. Since supply ships from Mexico arrived only sporadically, these officials and priests regarded such trade with the Bostonians as completely logical and moral.

So still more Boston vessels came, making Drake's Bay their base. Canoes took provisions to the hunters on the Farallon Islands and brought back furs. When Gov. Jose Arguello was informed that 130 canoes were operating between Bodega and San Francisco and were slipping into San Francisco Bay to hunt, he ordered a strict watch kept. The hunters circumvented this by portaging skins across the Marin Peninsula.

In 1811 a total of 8,118 otter skins was received at Sitka from California. The Russians, deciding that they wanted to extend and expand their own operations down the coast and try to make some commercial arrangements with the Spaniards, prepared to make Fort Ross their center for hunting and supplies. When orders arrived from Madrid to limit trade with the Russians to agricultural and manufactured products, Gov. Pablo Vicente de Sola launched a strict enforcement policy, as a result of which several Russians, Americans, and Aleuts were captured and imprisoned and a few sent to Mexico for trial on charges of illegal otter hunting.

From 1817 to 1820, the Russians continued attempts to get trading concessions from the Spaniards, but were never successful. Possibly as a result of this, they changed their own policy of making deals with the Americans. When, after the War of 1812, American vessels began hastening back to the Northwest for furs, the Russian-American Company declined to enter into further partnerships with them. So the Americans became "tramps," operating independently and picking up what they could.

Essentially, they were smugglers, and the Ortega Ranch at Refugio, west of Santa Barbara, became the center of the contraband trade. It was frequently staked out by the Santa Barbara authorities. "Never had so many Yankees been locked in Spanish jails, appeared before Spanish courts, and encountered Spanish officials," it was said. But when Capt. Eayrs' *Mercury* was boarded by armed men from a Spanish ship and he was taken to Monterey for trial, he testified that "the highest and lowest officers on the coast had entreated him to bring articles for cultivation, and the mission padres, articles of religion," for which he said he took his pay "in the produce of the land and a few otter furs."

James S. Wilcocks of the *Traveler,* a Yankee distributor of oriental wares and brother of the American consul in Canton, was fired on in Peru, where the ban on trading with foreigners was even more stringent than in California. He repaired his ship in Hawaii, put in at Santa Barbara, was permitted to buy a few supplies "but no otter skins." He sold some goods to Fr. Joaquin Pascual Nuez at San Gabriel, sailed south to Loreto, then came up to Monterey in June 1817, where he was refused supplies until he appealed to Gov. Sola, who again ordered "no skins."

When his vessel was seized for having contraband goods— otter skins, what else?—he pleaded that he was "clothing naked soldiers, and supplying vestments, ornaments, and tools to the padres."

IN 1822, when Mexico became independent of Spain, it rejected Spain's mercantile policy. Foreign vessels could then, for the first time legally, buy and barter for otter skins. Luis Antonio Arguello, acting governor of Mexican California, went into the business himself. In the Northwest, the supply had dwindled to almost nothing, so in 1823 the Russians were happy to sign a contract with Arguello which gave them the right to hunt anywhere from San Francisco to San Diego, splitting the proceeds.

Arguello bought a schooner, the *Rover,* from Capt. John Rogers Cooper, who had come out from Boston in 1823. Cooper agreed to remain on the vessel for a trip to the Orient, taking 300 otter skins and 300 tails, which brought $7,419 on the Canton market.

Aleuts were now hunting in Monterey Bay and had 429 more skins ready for Cooper when he made a second voyage in late 1824. Upon his return he found that Jose Maria Echeandia had been named governor and had adopted a much more restrictive policy.

Two-thirds of the crews now had to be Mexican citizens, and a legal duty had to be paid on every skin. Manuel Victoria, who succeeded Echeandia in 1830, was a believer in strict enforcement, which became even stricter the following year when otter hunting was limited to "hijos del pais" (citizens).

Echeandia had told the Mexican government that "the Russians always conducted themselves with the greatest delicacy and honesty, whereas the Americans hunted without ever asking for a license."

Cooper, naturalized as Juan Bautista Rogers Cooper, began hunting with an Echeandia license. William Goodwin Dana, also naturalized, hired an expert marksman, Isaac Galbraith, who had been with the Jedediah Smith overland expedition of 1826-27. On Santa Rosa Island Galbraith and two Kanaka assistants brought in up to 30 otters per week working without canoes. The gun, replacing the arrow and bone-tipped spear, was to speed the process of eliminating the otters.

Other Americans who had been beaver trappers like Galbraith were lured west by reports of a new fur wealth from the sea. Among them were James Ohio Pattie, George Yount, William Wolfskill, and Ewing Young.

Young made a deal to hunt otters for Mission San Gabriel on its vessel, the *Guadalupe*. Job Dye contracted with Fr. Luis Gil y Taboada of Mission San Luis Obispo, and Edward McIntosh joined him. Isaac J. Sparks and John Burton worked the Channel Islands, later joined by Dye. George Nidever, considered the outstanding hunter of the period, was joined by Daniel Sills, then by Allen Light, a Negro known as Black Steward. Nidever, Sparks, and Steward became naturalized citizens. Mexican wives could also obtain hunting licenses. Maria Josefa Boronda and Eduarda Osuna became legal hunters. As expert riflemen arrived in California in greater numbers, licensed citizens hired them.

The Mexicans, however, were beginning to worry about the tremendous reduction in the number of otters. "In order to conserve the species," under the mistaken notion that pups could survive without their mothers, pups were no longer to be killed. Licenses now specified where hunting of adult otters could be done. In 1831 Gov. Victoria had complained to Mexican officials that indiscriminate killing had become a serious problem. Gen. Mariano Vallejo ordered protective areas at the mouth of Petaluma and Sonoma creeks, which were shortly intruded upon and all the remaining otters killed.

During most of 1833 Juan B. R. Cooper had 12 baidarkas with Kodiak hunters operating along the central California coast. He had hired them from the Russians at Fort Ross. But like many mainland hunters, such as Juan Bautista Alvarado and Jose Castro, Cooper was infuriated that foreign merchants, mostly American residents of the Hawaiian Islands, were fitting out large ships to engage in illegal hunting along the California coastline, even equipping them with cannons. The first was the *Griffon,* with Capt. Charles Taylor, which had eight cannons and a crew of 24. In two months they obtained 300 sea otter skins between the Channel Islands and San Quintin in Baja California. On the next trip they obtained 80 skins in 12 days, but suddenly the otters were becoming scarce.

In December 1834 Gov. Jose Figueroa asked Mexico City for warships to break up the "invasion." Cooper was incensed by the "piratical manner" of ships from Hawaii whose crews stole cattle and mission horses. Northwest coast Indians, the Mexican government, and mainland huntsmen were all fighting the contrabandistas. Battles were breaking out on the Channel Islands between rival crews. In July 1836 Gov. Mariano Chico reported from Monterey that two brigs and one frigate, all smugglers, were hunting "in sight of all the world."

The "contrabandista war" continued until 1842, when the diminishing number of otters made it unprofitable for the merchantmen from Hawaii to continue to sail to California.

"Whereas there was taken 700 a few years ago, I took but 32 from San Francisco to Monterey and I do not think we shall get 600 skins on all the coast," Cooper wrote as early as 1832.

The logbook of the *Rover,* which came into the possession of Miss Frances Molera, Cooper's granddaughter, became one of the best information sources on this period.

In the late 1830s and early 1840s small groups of "empresarios," resident American merchants who had become Mexican citizens, continued to outfit ships which made short trips to the Channel Islands and the coast between Monterey and Santa Barbara, and which also explored the Baja California otter fields, especially Redondo and Cedros islands and San Quintin Bay. But returns were decreasing everywhere. In five months a Nidever schooner-rigged whaleboat with three canoes obtained 109 skins. That was 1839. In 1845 Marcelino Escobar of Monterey financed two canoes with six men, who found nothing until they reached Piedras Blancas and San Simeon, and then got only two otters in three months.

The slaughter of sea mammals did not begin or end with sea otters. From times beyond the reach of memory, primitives clubbed the friendly and trusting seals that came ashore in the same places, at certain seasons, year after year. Men dressed in waterproof sealskin clothes sewed with seal sinews, went out in sealskin canoes to harpoon small whales and dolphins. Through the middle ages, when European whalers roamed the north Atlantic, marine mammals were sought primarily for their flesh. Then burgeoning human populations began to demand more and more oil to light the lamps of Europe, and the emphasis on whaling and sealing shifted to oil rendered from the boiled down blubber. This early "energy crisis" depleted the whales and seals of temperate European waters, and most whalers then turned to northern waters on both sides of the Atlantic. As explorers led the way to the New World and to the oceans of the southern hemisphere, the boldest whalers and sealers followed. These extended voyages, often as hazardous to the men as to their animal victims, were made possible by stops en route on lonely coasts and isolated islands to replenish ships' stores with fresh seal meat and with seal oil for "butter," for lamp oil, and for greasing ships' gear.

To untrained eyes, the noisy jostling crowds of seals, elephant seals, sea lions, and fur seals were all "seals." All were stripped of

Northern elephant seals, *Mirounga angustirostris,* get their common name from the male's overdeveloped nose, the proboscis, which hangs down over the mouth. When the animal is excited, the nose is inflated with air and raised up, acting as a resonating chamber that amplifies the loud bellowing. Presumably, this impresses rival bulls. It does frighten humans, and in any case no one should approach too closely to such a big and potentially dangerous mammal. A large body, insulated by a thick covering of blubber, is the elephant seals'strategy for staying warm in cold waters. In addition, these large seals spend much time on land warming up, especially during the breeding season. The larger males, which may reach 18 feet and weight 6,000 pounds, are polygamous and gather a harem of smaller females that may measure about 9 feet. (J.A. Mattison, Jr.)

The Alaskan fur seal, *Callorhinus ursinus,* has a thermal blanket of fur, but the hairs are not as long and are only half as dense as those of the sea otter. Additional insulation against cold is provided by a generous layer of fat underlying the skin. (N.Y. Zoological Park)

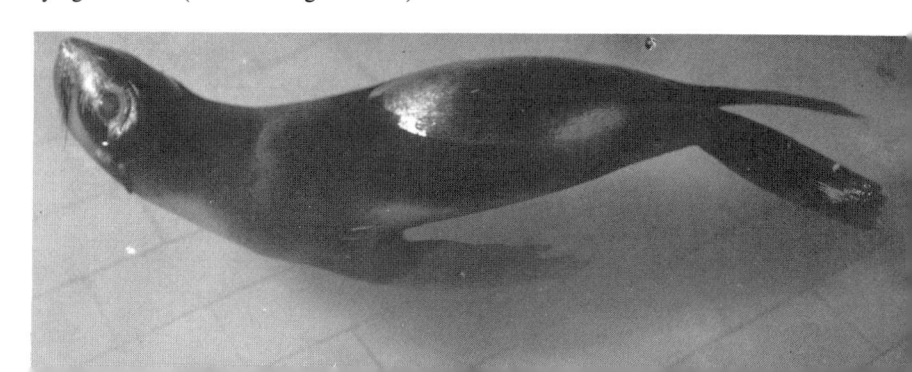

their blubber, which was rendered in large kettles or even in earthen pits filled with heated stones. The fur seals, whose soft and valuable underfur was disguised by a surface coat of coarse guard hairs, were killed with the others, for their blubber alone. When later the fur seal skins could be sold in China, at the port of Canton, they were shaved of their fur and the tanned hides made into luggage. Eventually the Chinese learned to properly prepare the velvety pelts of fur seals, but even then these continued to bring small change at a time when sea otter pelts were going for fabulous prices. Only when the sea otters were depleted, did the slaughter of millions of fur seals begin on a really large scale in the southern oceans and in the North Pacific.

The name "seal" can be applied to any fin-footed sea mammal, or pinniped. Strictly speaking, the pinnipeds called "fur seals" are not really seals at all, and neither are the "trained seals" of zoos and circuses, which are California sea lions. Fur seals and sea lions have long sinuous bodies, long necks, hind flippers that can be rotated forward, and small external ears. They are placed in the family Otariidae and separated from the "earless" or "true seals" like the harbor seals or the elephant seals. The fur seals should be called "sea bears," the name Steller gave them in 1742. It is an appropriate name for the furred animals now thought to be derived from a primitive land stock similar to that which gave rise to land bears.

Unfortunately, no story of any sea mammal can be said to have either a happy or an unhappy ending until the species is extinct. Only then is its fate certain and its status unchanging. Long considered extinct is the northern sea cow that fed Bering's starving men. Thereafter, Russians heading for the Aleutian Islands to hunt for sea otters, fur seals, and foxes, wintered on Bering Island to stock their larders with sea cow meat—not only because it came in large and placid packages, but because the flesh of the kelp-eating sea cow was tastier than than that of the carnivorous sea otters and fur seals. This huge mammal, now called *Hydrodamalis gigas,* was eaten to extinction by Russian fur-hunters in less than 30 years of its discovery by Bering's men. (The 1741 description and drawings sent by Steller are the sole account.) Vague reports and rumors of the sightings of animals generally thought to be extinct circulate now and then, and so it is with Steller's sea cow, but there are no verifications yet.

Wild animal furs are back in fashion with humans again, after almost two decades of "raised consciousness" about the extermination of land fur bearers. During those years "fake" (synthetic) furs were worn by even the most fashionable women. In the last few years, a declining fur industry, counting on a gradual loss of interest in environmentalism, has financed an expensive promotion of wild furs through advertising, brochures, and speaking tours directed to women's groups. Magazines in 1978 are suddenly replete with full-page ads for "wild fur" coats, including one of "wild Russian lynx" at $50,000. Those who cannot afford this will be offered good American raccoon, red fox, badger, muskrat, and skunk. Bobcat is not mentioned in most lists, but bobcat pelts are bringing more than $400 apiece, and those who thrilled to an occasional glimpse of a bobcat, even in populated areas like Carmel Valley, will in the future have to do without. For some time there has been talk of "culling" sea otters in California and of killing "surplus" sea otters in Alaska. Fur industry advertising speaks of "wild furs," "sports furs," and "fun furs," but it is too early yet to think about the name that will be given to sea otter fur, which may very well come from animals killed by a major oil spill—or from otters culled in Alaska under the provisions of the January 1979 waiver of the moratorium on the "taking" of Alaskan marine mammals. The quota for otters is up to 3000 annually.

An abalone is a kind of marine snail with an ear-shaped shell that has a very small spiral portion and a very large last whorl that contains most of the animal and covers all of the foot, even when it is extended. The slender, dark projections around the edge of the scalloped-edged mantle, are sensitive to food and to danger. When the animal withdraws its tender parts and clamps the shell tightly against the rock, the respiratory current enters under the edge of the shell and escapes through the oval openings. (R. Buchsbaum)

7

WHO IS EATING ALL THOSE ABALONES?

SEVERAL YEARS AGO I was called into the office of the late Franklin K. "Pete" Arthur, then editor of the *Monterey Peninsula Herald,* to interview four fishermen who were en route to Sacramento to demand some sort of action from the state legislature to protect abalone resources from the otters.

They charged that the otters had been challenging their means of subsistence by cleaning out every abalone they could reach, regardless of size, leaving only the smallest ones which were impossible to dislodge from inaccessible crevices. They wanted their side of the story told in every major newspaper they could contact. They were also carrying with them an exquisite small jade carving of an otter lying on its back, holding a fingernail-sized abalone shell on its chest. This was to be a present to their state senator.

Their spokesman was a noisy character who believed in addressing editors at the top of his lungs.

"You're not going to get any additional space by yelling at me," Pete told him. "Did it ever occur to you that the abalone may have been wiped out by overfishing, just like Monterey's sardines?"

This has been the point of view and conviction of such respected oldtimers as W. R. Holman of Pacific Grove, who recalled that in his youth, at the turn of the century, all the waterfront rocks of that city were so thick with abalones that it was almost impossible to walk on the rocks without stepping on them. The same was true all along the rocky portions of the Monterey Peninsula coastline. Then as the demand grew in the Orient for dried abalone meat, local entrepreneurs hired Chinese and Japanese fishermen and divers to scour every promontory and go deeper and deeper for the shellfish. Ships from the Orient stood by at Point Lobos and other loading spots and took aboard many millions of the abalones.

"Most of the abalones were gone long before the sea otters started making a comeback here," Mr. Holman said.

Commenting on the section "Indian-Sea Otter-Abalone Balance" in the Department of Fish and Game leaflet "The Sea Otter, *Enhydra lutris,*" archeologist Sylvia N. Broadbent points out that the section begins: "One of the more interesting aspects of sea otter interactions is the theoretical relationship between Indians, sea otters, and the invertebrates utilized by both."

"There was nothing theoretical about this relationship in any sense," she declared. "It was a real, historical fact. This may seem like a picayune sniping at words, but since the real historical facts flatly contradict the assertion made in the Introduction that 'within the sea otter's stabilized foraging range there can be virtually no human harvesting of abalones,' I think this evidence of sloppy thinking, if not deliberate tergiversation, is worth taking note of.

"The amount of abalone shell in Indian coastal middens from Humboldt to San Diego counties is simply fantastic ... especially on the Monterey Peninsula and in the San Luis Obispo and Santa Barbara areas.

"Moreover, the archeological and ethnohistorical evidence makes it quite clear that by no means all the abalone shell removed from the Pacific stayed in the coastal middens; it was an important item of trade, distributed far and wide, into Arizona and New Mexico, at least as early as 500 A.D., and all over the Great Plains in protohistoric times. It was an important material for beads and pendants in the Early Horizon of the Sacramento-San Joaquin Delta area from about 1000 B.C. on.

"In excavations I did at Carmel Mission in 1954 and 1955, we found just about the same concentration of abalone shell as occurs in prehistoric coastal sites. There, we know the whole deposit was accumulated between 1770 and about 1840—i.e., about 70 years. In one area it was over 6 feet deep. The average population was on the order of 300 to 500 persons. It is hard to see how that number of people could 'shorepick' that volume of abalone in that time under present conditions. And at the Mission the Indians had a lot of things to eat that weren't available in prehistoric times: beef and wheat, especially. And we also found a lot of remains of sea urchins, crabs, clams, oysters, mussels, barnacles, turban snails, chitons, and so forth. To the Indians, shellfish was what might be called a 'fall-back' food supply—what you ate between seasons when other foods were in short supply. It wasn't a rare gourmet delicacy, but a basic part of the food supply.

Otter bones, scattered over the surface or excavated from old Indian kitchen middens, provide part of the evidence for the taking of otters for food and for fur by the coastal Indians. (J.A. Mattison, Jr.)

"The argument that 'within the sea otter's stabilized foraging range there can be virtually no human harvest of abalones ... red crab ... rock crab ... sea urchins ...' etc., is historically absurd. Before European-inspired cataclysmic hunting of the otters, there *was* considerable human harvest of all these and other intertidal animals. It is very clear that the Indians flourished, the otters flourished, and so did abalones, sea urchins, crabs, mussels, chitons, oysters, clams, and so on and so forth."

According to Donald M. Howard, founder-president of the Monterey County Archaeological Society, who has presided over the excavation of innumerable digs along the county coastline, "The abundance of abalone in Indian middens refutes the idea that sea otters prevent human take of abalones. Indians were able to harvest vast numbers in competition with otters. It has been claimed that most of the abalones found in the middens were collected by Indians after storms.

"However, neatly formed whale-rib wedges used to pry off abalone are found with large shells, showing that the Indians selectively removed abalone. Characteristic Indian wedge scars found on the shell margins attest to this use of wedges. Giant and keyhole limpet shells also bear wedge scars. Several Indian skulls found at the Carmel site had fused ear orifices, an ailment of some modern skindivers, indicating that some Indians may have regularly obtained large abalone by free diving.

"We must conclude from an analysis of these valuable sites that otter predation did not prevent the Indians from obtaining, with wedges, impressive numbers of large abalone. Yet, Indian, otter, and abalone were once a balanced community. These aborigines did not misuse their resources."

Near Carmel, where otters offshore were probably dense in Indian times, one midden was shown, by radio-carbon dating, to represent 2400 years of continuous deposition of mollusc shells and other discarded skeletal parts. Abalone shells were abundant throughout the 20-foot deep accumulation. At Big Sur a comparable shell midden was estimated to represent 3700 years of Indian feasting.

Large abalone shells scattered over the surface of an unexcavated midden. Such shells are abundant in middens laid down when otters were about 10 times as numerous as they are now. (J.A. Mattison, Jr.)

THE California Department of Fish and Game (DFG), over the years, has been of many minds about who is eating all those abalones. Going back to an official DFG report, *The Abalones of California,* published in 1948, we read the views of Paul Bonnot of the DFG staff:

> The initial human population of the West coast of North America was relatively sparse; the culture late Stone Age. One store of food was the abalone, which was plentiful and easily procured. The shell supplied material for personal adornment and served as a medium of exchange. Exploitation was circumscribed by weather and natural indolence, and did not seriously affect an inherent abundance, maintained by the reproductive ability of the species. This state of affairs prevailed for thousands of years.
>
> The first [European] immigrants who came to the West Coast found natural resources so diverse and redundant that there was little incentive to make use of such a lowly form as the abalone, especially since most Causasians have a bias on the subject of eating snails. In the last 50 years the human population of the West Coast has increased phenomenally, and the abalone, eulogized and promoted by civic and financial interests, has become a culinary delicacy much appreciated by epicures. Under these circumstances the supply is not equal to the demand and legal restrictions have been necessary to curb commercial over-exploitation.
>
> The sport take, responsive to the above mentioned panegyries, has also gradually and steadily increased. Laws have been passed to regulate the noncommercial abalone hunters, but it is difficult to enforce them effectively. Sportsmen, and so-called sportsmen, have become so numerous that they infest the coastal areas on every low tide. They are so persevering in gratifying their acquisitive propensities, and many of them are so indifferent to legal restrictions or so lacking in a sense of probity that the abalone has virtually disappeared from the beaches.

Abalone diving, Point Lobos, 1916. As it became necessary to dive deeper and deeper for the abalones, the original Japanese system of using only goggles as gear, and long hooks to pry the abalones loose, gave way to the diving suit and helmet. (Photo below by L. Josselyn; P.M. Hathaway collection)

Abalone drying at Point Lobos, 1900. A photo found by W. Bryan in the Monterey County Library, shows part of the abalone operation at Whaler's Cove, Point Lobos.

Point Lobos abalone cannery at Whaler's Cove, about 1916. A visitors' parking lot now occupies the site of the building in the foreground. (L. Josselyn, P. M. Hathaway Collection)

Where the abalones went. This picture was taken at the Point Lobos Canning Company in February 1916, and shows some of the boxes of canned minced abalones on which the company established its reputation between 1906 and the late 1920s. In the background is the steam tank in which the canned abalone meat was cooked. (L. Josselyn; P.M. Hathaway collection)

Discarded abalone shells, Point Lobos. The pile of red abalones grew higher and higher outside the Point Lobos Canning Company buildings, during the early 1900s. (L. Josselyn; P.M. Hathaway collection)

In the good old days, two gentlemen in the beachwear of the day (1916) pry abalones from the tidepool rocks of Carmel Bay, using a knife and a section of metal car spring. (L. Josselyn; P.M. Hathaway collection)

In 1969 Karl Kenyon had this to say in his book, *The Sea Otter in the Eastern Pacific Ocean:*

> During 1963, abalone fishermen in San Luis Obispo County, California, complained that sea otters were destroying the abalone resource of that area. Claims of spectacular damage to abalone beds appeared in many newspapers. In response to these complaints a hearing was held at the City Hall, San Luis Obispo, on 19 November 1963. At this hearing Mr. Harry Anderson, Deputy Director of the California Department of Fish and Game, presented testimony to the California Senate Fact Finding Committee on Natural Resources. He compared commercial landings of abalones in certain areas before and after sea otters were present in these areas. In 1961 when sea otters were present "the catch was over 1,550,000 pounds, by far the largest catch of any year in the 10-year period." He indicated further that competition among abalone fishermen has increased greatly. In 1928 there were 11 licensed commercial abalone fishermen in California. The number has increased to 505 in 1963. Since the abalone resource is limited, it becomes apparent that the individual fishermen can expect to obtain fewer abalones than when competition among them was less. It was concluded that "all the evidence we have indicates that the sea otter has not seriously harmed or threatened the abalone resource."

Bonnot's strong language about sport divers is not used now in DFG publications or talks. In recent years it has been the sea otters that "infest" California shores, though between 1960 and 1972 there was a 250 percent increase in sportdiving days and a

Pounding abalones on Fisherman's Wharf. After "Pop Ernst" Doelter introduced the method of pounding the abalone steaks almost paper-thin and quick-frying them, the Point Lobos Canning Company could sell as much abalone as it could catch, according to co-founder A.M. Allan's children and grandchildren. Fisherman's Wharf, Monterey, 1934. (R. Buchsbaum)

400 percent increase in sport divers on commercial boat trips. During June 1 to 5, 1977, along the northern California coast between the Elk and the Gulala Rivers, the undermanned DFG did write 45 abalone violations. On a single day during that same period 2000 sport divers competed for the abalones that were still left in the more accessible half of that 35-mile coastline. Sportdiving now centers on the north coast; and though the more accessible coves have been stripped, abalones are reported to be abundant in isolated coves, where sportsmen may take 50 at a time though the bag limit is only 4. In hidden coves poachers may dive and cache hundreds of abalones that find their way to a black market at wholesale prices ranging up to $15 per pound for abalones that go to Japan.

IN A 1975 study, Theodore C. Tutschulte, himself a former commercial abalone fisherman and now a biologist and student of abalones, says that in the summer of 1965 he could frequently obtain the [then] sport limit of 5 legal-sized pink abalones on a single "breath of air (one 'free dive')." By 1972 it was difficult for him to find 5 legals in a 30-minute search using scuba. And further, "... the factor that is at present limiting the overall abundance of the pink [abalone] population ... is predation on older age groups by modern man, which results in reduction of recruitment." The 880 licensed commercial abalone fishermen in California in 1966 had declined to about 187 in 1978, yet so great has been the fishing pressure from these divers and the sport divers that the commercial abalone take has decreased from about 5.5 million pounds in 1957 to less than a viable commercial fishery, an estimated 1.3 million pounds, in 1977. And because the DFG feels responsible for bolstering this waning resource they have made several revisions in the fishing rules for both commercial and sports divers.

The story is complicated by the fact that there are not just one but at least 5 common species of abalones, all edible: the reds (preferred over all others), the pinks, the greens, the whites, and the blacks. They have slightly different habitats and compete for food and space. From a study by Tutschulte, we learn, for example, that green abalones are most abundant in water of high turbulence with refuges available, such as occur on rocky headlands with deep crevices. Pink abalones prefer shallow quiet waters of rocky shoreline and the leeward areas of offshore rocks. As the reds and pinks decrease by commercial overfishing, other species take their place and the divers shift successively from one species to another, disguising the near-exhaustion, in certain places, of the more preferred species. The DFG people are aware that without such information they cannot responsibly "manage" the natural "resources" and they carry out their own studies as well as cooperating with university biologists.

Abalones "shoulder to shoulder" cover the shore in the intertidal zone studied by Richard Burge, biologist from the Morro Bay DFG office. This photo taken in 1975 at San Nicolas Island shows an unnatural situation created by the extinction of the sea otter around these islands. What it does to the natural balance of kelps and other marine life is just beginning to be studied. (D. Miller)

Abalones and sea urchins compete for space on the bottom and for fragments of drift kelp on which both feed. The abalones in the left foreground have their shells covered with dense growths of calcareous plants, delicate hydroids, and bryozoan colonies, but the row of holes, through which the water current leaves the abalone are unobstructed and easily seen. Both urchins and abalones increased enormously on California shores during the decades when sea otters were nearly extinct, but this brought on changes that we now realize were unfavorable to kelps, and to the sport and commercial fishes that shelter in or feed on kelps. (California Dept. of Fish and Game)

A SIMILAR STORY can be told for commercial and sports clamming. Clams vary in numbers more than abalones do, and it is well known by local residents that there are good and bad years for clamming. One year there may be plenty of clams for thousands of people and the next year clams may be scarce. It takes from 3 to 9 years for a Pismo clam to grow to legal size, depending upon the average temperature and salinity of the water and other factors such as severe storms that may wipe out a given year class. In some years a clammer may dig his quota of 10 clams in an easy day's outing, but in another year come away disappointed with none. As with the abalone, there is a legal size limit for the Pismo clam. In 1978 the lower limit for Pismo clams in Monterey Beaches was 5 inches, and it takes 4 to 5 legal sized clams to make 1 pound of meat. As with abalones, people frequently overestimate size when picking and then throw away the sublegals (if they fear detection). Those discarded clams not already destroyed by the digging forks die anyway. Clam mortality is also caused by oil and other pollutants. Besides, predators other than humans love clams; these include rays, surf fishes, crabs, moon snails, gulls, and sea otters.

In 1964 the legal bag limit for the Pismo clam was 10 clams. At that time the human population of California was about 10 million; in 1979, the bag limit is still 10 clams and the human population is over 20 million.

The DFG booklet, *The Pismo Clam,* informs its readers that from 1916 to 1947, when commercial digging of Pismo clams was allowed, about 100,000 pounds (50,000 clams) were taken each year by commercial diggers alone; 666,000 pounds in 1918. Following the discussion of clam attrition from commercial sources, the booklet takes up sports fishing:

> The noncommercial digger (sportsfisherman) has probably contributed even more to the losses incurred in the Pismo clam population. During a single weekend noncommercial clam diggers were checked off Pismo and Morro beaches at all exits. Over 75,000 pounds of clams accompanied these clammers. Probably twice as many undersized clams were left exposed by the carelessness of these diggers. During a

2½month period some 2,000,000 clams (4 million pounds) were taken from a four-mile stretch of Pismo Beach. Untold thousands of others were either severely injured by clam forks or left exposed on the sand to be washed ashore by the incoming tide, there to die.

From the annual census a mortality rate was determined for five-inch clams at Pismo Beach. Fifty-five percent of the clams died in their first year; 45 percent of the remainder died the second year, and 29 percent of the balance died the third year. The fourth year the mortality rate jumped to 34 percent as a few "just a wee bit too small but I'll take it anyway" clams, along with some which had attained legal size, entered the catch. The next three years, as even more clams attained the then legal size of five inches the mortality rate jumped to 52 percent, 68 percent, and 72 percent respectively. ... The size limit of four and one-half inches will allow many more clams to be utilized.

HOWEVER, by 1978, the DFG, hard put to protect dwindling shellfish resources argued that it is required and committed to protect all of California's marine resources, including otters, fish, and shellfish, and that this can be done only by a management program that will manage fishes, crabs, abalones, clams, and sea otters—not to mention the commercial and sports fishermen.

ASKED TO COMMENT on this, Dr. Betty Davis replied: "The DFG is the only organization in the state that is staffed, equipped, and funded to protect all of California's marine resources. And I wish they could! But the DFG receives more than 90 percent of its funding from licenses and inevitably comes to look on license buyers—the commercial fishermen, the sports fishermen, and the kelp-cutters—as their major clients. In turn, having paid their fees, the license buyers expect that the DFG will 'do something' about the declining catch of overfished resources. And, so do the legislators in Sacramento when harried by their constituents.

"The human population of California is expanding at an unprecedented rate, while the slow-growing populations of clams and abalones have been programmed, through millions of years of natural selection, to remain relatively stable—except for occasional ups and downs caused by changes in physical conditions. When 150,000 humans turn out for a single low tide at Pismo Beach, collecting huge numbers of clams and throwing back even greater numbers of sublegals to be eaten by gulls or to dessicate in the sun, the clam population suffers. Some clam beaches have had to be closed by the DFG for at least as long as 12 years in order for recovery to take place. The otters were north of such beaches at the time of closure, and are still north of most of these clamming beaches, so the decline here is due to factors other than otters—with human pressures playing an obvious role. However, where small numbers of otters have moved north and joined clamdiggers at Sunset Beach in Santa Cruz county, the decline there is attributed to an 'otter foraging spree' (interview with DFG, *Monterey Peninsula Herald,* October 16, 1975).

"The truth is that the DFG is in an untenable position, and an uncomfortable one. As the number of license buyers keeps rising, the number of fishermen taking their catch from the same bowl of shellfish increases—and the size of their individual take soon decreases. Yet, there is little the DFG can do to change the reproductive habits or slow natural growth rates of clams and abalones. In addition to increasing human pressure, shellfish also suffer from related human impacts such as pollution, smothering by tons of sewage sludge, harbor dredging, and shore changes induced by piers and other structures. Surely, no one in the DFG really believes that we can return to the high yields that characterized earlier times when there were far fewer people in California.

"It is unfortunate that the DFG raises the hopes of clammers and abalone divers by implying that as soon as the DFG can regain management of sea otters, the shellfisheries will be saved and there may ensue greater abundance of clams, abalones, and crabs for all. It is also too bad that the DFG doesn't inform fin fishermen about the positive effects otters have on kelp forests and very likely on the fin fish fisheries found in such forests. All available evidence suggests that the return of sea otters is restoring a more balanced ecosystem, with fewer abalones and urchins, perhaps, but more kelp-dependent fishes. Sea otters eat a great variety of animals that feed on kelp: snails, kelp crabs, limpets, sea urchins, and abalones among them. Abalones and urchins generally eat fragments of kelp that drift by, but if kelps are damaged by pollution or overcutting and the supply diminishes, sea urchins attack the living kelp. As kelp beds are decimated by urchins, abalones and fishes decline. Where sea otters abound, and control such grazers, kelp beds thrive—and so do the nearshore sport and commercial fishes that shelter and feed in kelp forests. It is interesting to note that of five nearshore habitats along the coast of California that were assessed by the DFG before the siting of a Liquified Natural Gas (LNG) terminal on the shoreline, the site with otters had far more rockfishes, abalones, and urchins than any of the other four.

"A recent paper by Simenstad, Estes, and Kenyon in *Science,* of 28 April 1978, reports 'dramatic' differences in kelps and associated fish populations in Alaskan waters with and without otters. These authors conclude that 'dense populations of sea otters in the western Aleutian Islands limit sea urchins to sparse populations of small individuals. In turn, this interaction is important to the maintenance of robust kelp beds and a rich associated fauna of fishes, birds, and marine mammals.'

"To add to the conflict between its clients, the DFG licenses kelp-cutting with negotiable limits on the number of times a year these ecologically invaluable kelp forests can be cut.

"To satisfy the conflicting resource claims of all these exploitive interest groups—shellfishermen, fin fishermen, and kelp harvesters—is more than the DFG can manage. But seizing on the restriction of sea otters as a panacea in their sea of troubles is not the answer and may pose a threat to this very valuable nonconsumptive resource. Rather, the DFG should be busy worrying about how to regulate and reduce fishing impacts and about how to protect the extraordinarily vulnerable sea otter from the oil spills that are sure to come. An animal so central to the health of the kelp forests, and all their associated inhabitants, deserves restitution not restriction, by the DFG. The otter should not be used as a scapegoat for overfishing by a burgeoning human population.

"In Mexico, where there are no otters, the abalone landings declined by 43 percent between 1968 and 1973; and the total landings of California's commercial fishery declined an identical 43 percent about the same time, 1968 to 1974."

DR. RALPH BUCHSBAUM adds, "sea otters do indeed eat abalones. But even where otters have been long established, and are near equilibrium density, as in the area around Hopkins Marine Station, they continue to come up frequently with large abalones. They also eat a great variety of other invertebrates, so that they do not "clean out" the abalone stocks as intensive commercial or sports collecting tends to do. The DFG is fond of saying that the presence of sea otters "precludes" a commercial abalone fishery. But twice in the past, heavy commercial abalone fishing in Monterey Bay precluded a continuing commercial abalone fishery. In recent years commercial yields in California have come mainly from the Channel Islands off southern California. How long such areas will last we can only guess. A substantial portion of the abalones eaten in California restaurants are now imported from the rapidly declining Mexican fishery.

"Leaving sea urchins to the otters would be the most trouble-free way of relieving some of the predation-pressure on abalones and maintaining a natural balance among kelps, urchins, otters, and abalones that in the past lasted for millions of years. But the Japanese have depleted their urchins, and their abalones; and, moreover, their yen has lately risen in relation to the dollar. So California sea urchins have been going to the Japanese trade—only 200 pounds in 1971 and a whopping 13.7 million pounds in 1977, according to the latest figures from the DFG.

"The oriental trade once finished off the commercial abalone fishery of the Monterey Bay, and now the squids *(Loligo opalescens)* that breed prolifically in Monterey Bay are about to follow. Until a year or so ago squids could be bought for 25 cents a pound on the Monterey wharf. In 1978 they sold for 50 cents a pound, but the price of this "poor man's abalone" is about to rise sharply as the supply starts going mostly overseas.

"In a November 5, 1978 article in the *Monterey Peninsula Herald,* Chad Lincoln states that on an exceptional night, a boat in Monterey Bay can fill the hold with nearly 50 tons of squids. And he continues:

> With a season that runs nearly half a year, and increasing demand at home and abroad luring more and more boats to make more catches, will the squid go the way of the sardine and become just a memory for Monterey Bay? Not everyone is convinced that the sardine disappeared as a result of excessive harvesting. But the squids appear in mass in fairly shallow water during spawning and are extremely vulnerable. It seems only logical then that greater numbers of well-placed nets inevitably must have some effect on the future generations of this mollusk.
>
> Not to worry at this point, says the State Department of Fish and Game; not to worry, say the fishermen. So, let's not worry. Enjoy this delectable sea food, the surrogate abalone, which still is the best bargain in the fish market.

"The October issue of *Pacific Search* explains 'Why Salmon Costs So Much' in an article by Boyd A. Levet. Part of the answer is that a Seattle-based fish company has just signed a deal to expand its exports to a Japanese company by $100 million over the next three years. Pacific salmon from our West Coast goes also to Europe now that the franc and mark are up in relation to the dollar. The price of salmon is skyrocketing, and salmon is joining abalone as luxury food.

"There is talk of keeping salmon fisheries viable with expanded state hatchery programs and ocean ranching by large corporations. There seems to be no way of narrowing the gap between the natural supply of abalones and the ever-increasing number of human abalone eaters except through an expansion of current attempts at mariculture. Imagine trying to supply 220 million Americans with wild turkeys or wild mushrooms from the woods and fields! Culturing abalones, at present, is a difficult, expensive, and risky venture. After years of large capital out-lays on research into methods of raising abalones, a few of the most successful private groups are within sight of selling 3 to 4-inch abalones to Japan, where they bring a price most Americans will not pay. George Lockwood, at Monterey, is also beginning to supply one-centimeter abalones to the DFG, which is trying to restock the California coast with abalones. Unfortunately, these small abalones (see photo page 109) are often gobbled up by fishes or octopuses before they can find a rock crevice in which to hide.

"The U.S. appears to be shaping its economy to resemble that of a third-world country—exporting raw materials (seafoods, wheat, soybeans, raw logs, coal, etc.) and importing manufactured goods such as automobiles and television sets."

Female sea otter eating an abalone after presenting the shell to her young pup, who played with it. This mother and her nursing pup (see photos in chap. 4) were observed and photographed daily by admiring crowds of otter-watchers on the Coast Guard Pier at Monterey. She appeared next to the pier, usually between 8 and 10 a.m., during February and March of 1978. Another mother and pup have appeared in the same area in February 1979. Some 1978 watchers came in regularly from the far reaches of Carmel Valley, and at least one came from as far away as Fresno. The pleasure afforded thousands of otter-watchers depletes neither abalones nor otters and brings economic benefits to the merchants of California shores that far exceed the income derived from commercial collecting or from the serving of increasingly rare and expensive abalone steaks to a few diners. (R. Buchsbaum)

Preparing squids for dinner is still an economical way to enjoy seafood in the Monterey Bay Area, but perhaps not for long if the local supply starts to go mostly overseas, along with abalones. At least, no one will blame the otters for the decline in California squids. (R. Buchsbaum)

Egg masses of a sea urchin are a delicacy in many parts of the world. They are exposed by cutting off the upper half of the globular shell and are then ladled out with the tongue by real aficionados. In California sea urchins were left mostly to the sea otters, except for a few eaten by immigrants of Mediterranean background and those used by biologists at marine laboratories for studies of fertilization and embryonic development of the eggs. (R. Buchsbaum)

8

ARGUMENTS FROM THE DFG

A T A MEETING of the California State Fish and Game Commission held in January 1975 in San Diego, a draft report was presented on "Recent Abalone Research in California with Recommendations for Management," by Richard Burge, Steven Schultz, and Melvyn Odemar. The DFG report stated that while recognizing that "excessive picking pressure on sublegal abalones and improper size limits" have contributed to the decline of the commercial abalone landings, none of its recommendations for reduced seasons, reduced bag limits, and size limits "will provide for harvestable resource in the presence of an unrestrained population of sea otters. Therefore, in the absence of sea otter management, abalone management programs can only be effective until the areas are populated by the expanding sea otter population."

"When the Endangered Species Act was passed in 1973, the U.S. Fish and Wildlife Service agreed with us that the sea otter was not threatened," said Daniel J. Miller, senior marine biologist in the Operations Research Branch of DFG in Monterey. "Unfortunately, politics has since got into the decision-making and arbitrary interpretations of the data are being made."

Despite Miller's statements, conservationists point out that the southern sea otter is listed as a threatened mammal in *Threatened Wildlife of the U.S.A., 1973,* published by the U.S. Fish and Wildlife Service, and that the "arbitrary interpretations" he refers to were made by mammalogists of that service and the Marine Mammal Commission and its scientific advisory board.

"We don't agree that the southern sea otter is a separate subspecies," Miller continued. "We say that it's the same as the Alaskan variety. But we're considering our population as if no other existed. We feel that this population is safe, not threatened, but we need to conduct research to show that containing the animal in a certain range won't hurt the population. We have a responsibility to protect all wildlife. And while protecting the otters we must protect and enhance the fisheries that the otters would otherwise preclude."

THE QUESTION of whether the southern sea otter can be considered a separate subspecies, *Enhydra lutris nereis,* has been a subject of major controversy between the DFG and the Friends of the Sea Otter, an organization of scientists, teachers, and concerned citizens which has carried on a constant battle to protect the southern sea otter and facilitate its comeback. The most consistent physical differences between the northern and southern sea otters involve certain features of the skull. In 1971 Dr. Aryan I. Roest found that otter samples from the Aleutian Islands and California were separable at a level of better than 90 percent on the basis of skull structure. Later he found that specimens from southern Alaska were intermediate between the two extremes, so he changed his conclusions and decided that both belonged to a single subspecies.

The DFG adopted this point of view, stating in an official publication in 1974 that "Now that *E. lutris nereis* is no longer valid, the question of sea otters in California being rare or endangered is void inasmuch as there are over 120,000 sea otters now extant in Alaskan waters, and over 1,600 in California."

In October 1975, in a paper published by the California Academy of Sciences, "The Taxonomic Status of the Southern Sea Otter," Drs. John Davis and W. Z. Lidicker, Jr., reexamined Roest's data and the available literature and suggested an alternative interpretation. "In our opinion," they stated, "the known facts strongly support the conclusion that the southern sea otter should continue to be recognized as a separate subspecies *(E. lutris nereis)*. ... At present a 1,700-mile gap (between Alaska and California) exists within this vast range." They pointed out that (1) no skulls were examined from this section between Prince William Sound and Monterey; of 16 skulls from Prince William Sound, the southeastern Alaskan locality, 12 were of the Californian type, suggesting that a southern subspecies may once have extended far north, intergrading with a northern subspecies in southern Alaska; (2) the present southern population is completely isolated and does not exchange genetic material with any other sea otter population; (3) because it was reduced to such a tiny remnant, the genetic constitution of the southern population may have become considerably altered; (4) there appear to be behavioral differences between northern and southern sea otters, especially in terrestrial locomotion and reproductive behavior: the northern otters bear their young on land; the southern, in the water.

"Nomenclature, to be effective, should reflect the natural biological situation as accurately as possible," Dr. Davis wrote in *The Otter Raft* in December 1975. "In my opinion, there are a number of disadvantages in considering the northern and southern sea otters as belonging to a single subspecies. ... The recognition of a northern subspecies, *Enhydra lutris lutris,* and a southern subspecies, *E. lutris nereis,* would reflect the natural situation much more accurately."

In his book *North American Recent Mammals, 1975,* Dr. E. Raymond Hall of the Museum of Natural History, University of Kansas, lists three sea otter subspecies: *Enhydra lutris gracilis,* ranging from the southern tip of the Kamchatka Peninsula south, originally to the northern shore of Honshu; *Enhydra lutris lutris,* from the end of the Aleutian Islands chain, along the islands and coast to Vancouver, B.C.; and *Enhydra lutris nereis,* from the Straits of Juan de Fuca, southward along the coast to Sebastian Vizcaino Bay, Baja California.

IN 1974 the DFG proposed that the southern sea otter range be restricted to the area between Cayucos and Seaside. Unacceptable to conservationists and hotly protested, this was subsequently extended in a 1976 proposal from Avila, San Luis Obispo County, to Miramontes Point, San Mateo County. The department's 1976 objectives were: "To provide an adequate number of sea otters for maintenance of a healthy, self-sustaining population in areas where they will receive minimum adverse human impact and provide ample opportunities for public observation and scientific study; to restrict the distribution of the sea otter to protect the state's remaining recreational and commercial shellfish fisheries; and to enable possible development of marine aquaculture in coastal waters."

The DFG also wanted to make sea otters "available to scientific institutions for research on physiology, pathology, medical care, husbandry, food habits and behavior, and available for public display in oceanariums, subject to federal requirements for such."

Studies would include "the development of new and improved capture techniques, tagging methods, translocation techniques and care of animals held in captivity; population parameters including birth and death rates, sex ratios, age composition, habitat requirements, distribution and numbers, movements and social interactions."

Contracts would provide for "necropsies of all fresh carcasses recovered; histopathology, establishment of a serum bank and determination of pollutant assimilation."

Research would also determine "long-term impact of sea otter foraging upon coastal ecosystems, including intensive baseline and food web studies in the bull kelp forest ecosystem near Avila and in the giant kelp forest system near Santa Cruz."

Avila was chosen by the DFG as the southern periphery of the proposed otter range "to establish a viable population of sea otters to the south of the oil terminal at Estero Bay ... and to protect valuable shellfish resources south of Shell Beach, especially the Pismo clam fishery. "Without containment," stated the DFG proposal, "sea otters could move into the Pismo Beach area in from two to four years."

The proximity of Avila Harbor, it was said, "presents easy access to the area for tagging operations and other studies. The area off Shell Beach can be utilized as a convenient capture site for sea otters that migrate south of Avila."

Miramontes Point was similarly chosen "to establish a viable population north of the Moss Landing oil terminal facilities, to protect the valuable shellfish fisheries in the Gulf of the Farallons and north to Oregon."

Nearby Princeton was proposed as the base of DFG boat operations, and the kelp habitat off Pillar Point "to facilitate capture of animals before they reach valuable resource areas."

Miller estimated (in mid-1977) that it would take the "migrant front" of otters from 8 to 10 years to arrive at Miramontes Point. This would allow plenty of time for proposed research, he said, including tagging young animals throughout the range to see where they were moving to and determining the rate of population increase accurately.

A grant had been made, he said, to the University of California at Santa Barbara to make a subtidal survey to determine the total effect of sea otter foraging on resources. An annual survey of Pismo clams was also to be made.

"If you're going to have both otters and shellfish fisheries, zones must be established," said Miller. "You can't have both in the same place. If the public decides it wants to save sport and commercial fishing of abalone, crabs, Pismo clams, sea urchins, lobsters, and Dungeness crabs, then some adjustments will have to be made, because otters remove 90 percent of what humans want, foraging from the accessible intertidal zone to a depth of at least 120 feet."

JOSEPH H. CONNELL, professor of zoology at U.C. Santa Barbara, writing to State Assemblyman Gary Hart, commented that "the reduction of abalone landings in recent years is a classic example of overfishing. The fact that they have also declined on the offshore islands of Southern California eliminates both 'environmental degradation' and the sea otter as possible causes of the decline. Overfishing pressure is by far the most reasonable explanation for the decline and the future of the fishing will be assured only by reduction in (1) the number of fishermen, particularly the novices who are probably responsible for most of the handling losses, (2) the length of the season, and (3) the total landings allowed."

"MAN DOES overexploit a resource and cut it down," Miller conceded. "But when otters move in, they reduce it beyond consumption levels. They're extremely efficient. Their whole behavior, way of life, and body functions are concerned with this cleaning out of food. A 50-pound otter will consume 5,000 to 8,000 calories per day, or three times what the average human consumes.

"Since they have to eat constantly in order to live, the population is forced to spread out. Every kelp bed is gone over every day. The dominant ones steal from the subdominant.

"People who think that we're plotting against the sea otters just don't understand the problem. And it's very difficult to convince them, since so much misinformation has been given out. This has become a tremendously emotional thing. For 25 or 30 years the fishermen have been after us to get rid of the otters. At times, reason has been lost.

"But we're determined to be objective. We want the public to be correctly informed. We have an obligation to show the people so that they can make an intelligent choice."

It is Miller's contention that when the fur traders reduced the number of otters so drastically, invertebrate fisheries flourished and man got used to utilizing them with no restraints. "Pismo clams used to be harvested with harrows drawn by teams of horses," he said. "When the otters staged their comeback, people were accustomed to having no competition for the seafood. Suddenly, it was in short supply. So how do you fix the blame and what do you do about it?"

HOWEVER, as recently as 1974, conservationists point out, in discussing a beach closure just north of Pismo Beach not yet reached by otters, John Fitch of the DFG stated: "Studies show that, without the closure, approximately 65 percent of the young clams at Atascadero Beach would die before reaching the legal minimum size of 4½ inches. Half of this loss would be caused by injuries inflicted by clam diggers." Other beaches near the same area were closed to all digging during a 12-year period from 1962-1974. These beaches had not been reached by otters, and the closures were obviously the result of human impact.

During the last few years, major oil spills at sea have been regarded by the conservationists, the Fish and Wildlife Service, and the Marine Mammal Commission as one of the greatest threats to the sea otter. As part of its contingency plan to offset an oil spill, the DFG has proposed "to extend sea otter distribution both north and south of two major oil terminals at Moss Landing and Estero Bay, precluding the possibility of a catastrophic oil spill endangering the population."

Such a spill, nevertheless, would result in oil sinking to the bottom and killing much of the otter's food, thus starving them, the conservationists argue. Also, they add, otters north and south of the oil terminals would still be too close and are known to be principally young males, which cannot be considered a viable breeding colony.

According to the DFG, there have been no otter deaths attributable to pollution from pesticides, heavy metals, or oil pollution in California, and no evidence that sewerage contaminants are affecting reproduction.

Some scientists assert that there is insufficient evidence to support this claim, and that the possibility of such pollution causing death can certainly not be ruled out. Whether or not otter deaths have been "attributed" to these factors means nothing, the conservationists argue further. Many otters washed up with no apparent cause of death could have been killed in this way, and certainly evidence of various pollutants in otter tissues makes this possibility of great concern.

The DFG concedes that "maintenance of an unpolluted habitat is one of the most important considerations of sea otter management," and in its "Proposal for Sea Otter Protection and Research," states that "greatly increased exposure to pollutants will occur if sea otters enter San Francisco Bay and certain mainland areas south of Point Conception," this being seen as one more argument in favor of restricting the otter's range.

Conservationists see the DFG proposal as confining the otter breeding stock between two oil tanker ports. And they are hesitant, they say, to turn over the management of sea otters to those who, as late as 1977, tended to discount the threat of oil spills to otters (see page 126).

There is another major item of disagreement between the DFG and its critics. Essentially sea otters are nonmigratory; there is no seasonal behavioral pattern, the DFG states, though acknowledging that there is no guarantee that translocated animals will remain where they are released.

It is not true that sea otters have no seasonal behavioral pattern, the conservationists declare; there is a well-known pattern of movement. During breeding periods the males that have been out on the peripheral portions move back into the more central portions of the range.

When the proposed range from Avila to Miramontes Point is fully occupied, one of three decisions will have to be made, the DFG declares:

(1) Cease translocation. Allow sea otters to eventually occupy the entire California coastline.

(2) Recommend transplantation to establish an isolated second population, using extralimital animals.

(3) Reduce numbers by culling or reducing the reproductive

rate. The basic goal is to set up an experimental management regime that "can be tested in terms of husbandry of the animal."

The DFG foresees an eventual maximum population of 16,000 sea otters along all the California coastline and offshore islands. There could be die-offs of as many as 2,000 per year "to match annual reproduction in a saturated maximum-level population" due to injury of animals in the heavily congested harbors of Southern California and in San Francisco Bay. "Pups would probably be most endangered."

These 16,000 sea otters, the DFG predicts, "would consume 40,000 tons of shellfish annually. Otters would also preclude mariculture practices in ocean waters" and would wipe out recreational fisheries "with an estimated worth of $6,800,000."

Law enforcement, care of injured animals, necropsies, problems of starving pups, monitoring of population levels, distribution, and research "all would fall on the federal government" under the 1977 "threatened species" ruling, the department said.

Since the DFG had no wish to relinquish its own jurisdiction, it proposed that management authority be transferred to the state of California, "which would need funding for equipment and additional personnel." The alternative, the DFG said, would be to establish a cooperative program, state and federal.

Dr. Ralph Buchsbaum contends that the foregoing figures are unrealistic, as "there is not sufficient evidence to predict a maximum or even a probable future population. At the present rate of increase of 1.5 percent, the California sea otter population has a doubling time of about 47 years; it would take about 150 years to reach 16,000. Therefore, it is irresponsibly alarmist to warn that there would be 16,000 otters which would consume 40,000 tons (think of it as 80,000,000 pounds) of shellfish annually, with an estimated worth of $6,800,000. In 150 years, at (dare we predict?) a 7 percent annual rate of inflation, this would amount to $174,000,000,000! It is foolish to project such figures so long into the future—we just don't know enough about the rate of increase of the sea otter, the dynamics of the kelp forest ecology, the status of mariculture (for all we know, abalones will be raised in Chicago!), and the price of anything.

"One thing is certain: the doubling of California's human population since 1948, additional leisure time, and new technological advances in both commercial and recreational equipment have resulted in increased human invasion of the marine subtidal environment, with an impact of no small dimensions."

Commercial collecting of abalones produced modern middens that, in past decades, grew faster than the rate at which the shells could be bagged and sold to souvenir dealers and jewelry makers. (Burdette White)

9

FRIENDS OF THE SEA OTTER

IN 1968 the Friends of the Sea Otter (FSO), a trust and nonprofit organization, was co-founded by Margaret Owings of Big Sur and Dr. James Mattison, Jr. of Salinas. She became its president. From their home, *Wild Bird*, on a promontory of the rugged Big Sur coast, Mrs. Owings and her husband, internationally noted architect Nathaniel A. Owings, can see the otters in their daily life pattern, effortlessly moving to the rhythm of the sea.

A former member of the California State Parks Commission and a dedicated and articulate activist on the conservation front, Margaret Owings saw the need for a group which would have a single theme: the sea otter and its welfare along the California coast. Now more than 4,000 members from 48 states and five foreign countries follow the FSO activities and receive its publication, *The Otter Raft*.

The advisory board of the FSO is made up of a formidable contingent of scientists, doctors, lawyers, divers, and photographers. Among them are Alan Baldridge, naturalist and librarian at Hopkins Marine Station; William Bryan of Salinas, attorney, skilled underwater photographer and coproducer of the color film *Otters, Clowns of the Sea;* Dr. Ralph Buchsbaum of Pacific Grove, retired professor of zoology, University of Pittsburgh, author of the biology textbook *Animals without Backbones,* invertebrate ecologist, publisher; Mildred Buchsbaum, ecologist and invertebrate zoologist; Wymberley Coerr of Monterey, former member of the U.S. diplomatic service, treasurer of FSO; Dr. Betty Davis of Carmel Valley, research associate in zoology, Museum of Vertebrate Zoology, University of California, Berkeley, and research associate in parasitology, Hooper Foundation, UC School of Medicine, San Francisco, executive secretary of FSO; Dr. John Davis of Carmel Valley, director, Hastings Natural History Reservation, University of California; Capt. Elgin Hurlbert, USN, retired, of Pacific Grove, former president, Monterey Bay chapter, National Audubon Society; Dr. William Francis, biologist, retired from the U.S. Fish and Wildlife Service; James Mattison, Jr., M.D., of Salinas, surgeon, underwater naturalist, producer of the documentary color film *Back from Extinction;* Charles Mehlert, assistant director, Monterey area, California Department of Parks and Recreation, underwater parks specialist; Dr. Kenneth Norris, professor of natural history, UC Santa Cruz; Dr. Robert Orr, biologist and retired associate director, California Academy of Sciences, San Francisco; Margaret Owings, president of FSO, winner of the U.S. Department of the Interior's Conservation Service Award in 1975; Dr. John Pearse, professor of biology, UC Santa Cruz; Dr. John Phillips, biologist and biochemist, professor emeritus, Stanford University; Dr. James W. Rote, professor of marine sciences, expert on pollution, Moss Landing Marine Laboratory and faculty at UC Santa Cruz; Dr. Thomas Williams, veterinarian, Monterey; and Judson Vandevere, Monterey, FSO sea otter researcher.

A pamphlet issued by the Friends of the Sea Otter, *Who We Are and What We Believe,* expresses succinctly the purpose and future goals:

"Friends of the Sea Otter has steadily carried out research on the otter and stood alert to guard against actions detrimental to its welfare. It has encouraged public education to develop a sound conservation program. . . .

"Our concern is for the enhancement of a healthy sea otter population along the California coast, while the California Department of Fish and Game is essentially concerned with harvestable resources which serve commercial and sport opportunities. Although their attention includes the sea otter, they must listen to numerous conflicting points of view, including those from self-seeking shellfish interests. For this reason, and because license fees are the main source of revenue for the department, they view the sea otter primarily as a predator in competition with people and one to be managed where conflicts arise.

"Our basic disagreement lies here. For we regard the sea otter as a resource to be valued in its own right, one with an important role in promoting the enrichment and diversity of the marine ecosystem. We believe that the otters appear to be regulating their own affairs as well as can be expected in an environment subject to invasion and influence by man, and we feel they should be allowed to continue along their way, as far as possible, with a minimum of human interference."

In past years the FSO has also questioned the methods adopted by DFG in reaching an annual estimate of the sea otter population along the California coastline. Said Dr. Betty Davis, spokesperson for both the FSO and for California chapters of the Sierra Club on the subject of sea otters, "After an aerial count and a land count were made and the figures checked against one another to eliminate duplication, some numbers were dropped into the hat to allow for the animals which were assumed to have been missed for one reason or another. The 'allowable' percentage added was based on subjective correction factors for weather conditions, visibility, and fatigue of observers, and extrapolations were made. The final census figures given always were interpreted as indicating 'a rapidly expanding otter population.' We didn't agree.

"For example, from 1969 to 1972, aerial head counts showed 1,014, 1,040, 959, and 1,060 otters respectively, but estimates for the same years rose steadily: 1,352, 1,536, 1,598, and 1,631. In 1973 a new procedure of coordinated land/air counts was instituted, resulting in a little more accuracy.

"This procedure was refined, reaching its culmination in the 1976 count when kelp beds were mapped and a large team of ground observers checked on aerial counts. In 1976 the head count was tallied at 1,561 freeswimming otters and the estimate was 1,789; added to the latter was an estimated 67 clinging pups. Thus, whereas in 1973 the estimate was 1,711 on the basis of 1,146 counted, in 1976 it was 1,856 on the basis of 1,561 counted. From these figures it is apparent that the earlier estimates were indeed out of line. It is difficult to be sure how much of a 'guesstimate' the latest figure is, but it is certainly more accurate than previous figures. One thing is sure: due to the subjectiveness and inconsistencies of earlier counts, this most recent figure cannot be compared with previous figures used by the DFG to indicate an otter 'population explosion.' Population growth of the sea otter is slow. A mature female probably bears a pup only once in two years. And in addition to the usual attrition of pups there is also depredation by humans."

No otter census was conducted in 1977. But in 1978 the DFG spoke of stabilization of the otter population, then about 1800-1900, with migrant fronts not changing significantly.

Conceding that the otter's high metabolic rate requires daily food intake of about 20 to 25 percent of its body weight, the FSO declares that "the otter must be allowed to move along the coast as its food requirements dictate. Sea urchins, abalones, crabs, and mussels as well as some 40 other items in the kelp and on the ocean floor are favorites of the sea otter. Since kelp beds nurture and protect a vast community of marine life which is dependent upon them—and since urchins destroy the rootlike holdfasts of kelp—the otter's role in controlling urchins provides an illustration of the important interrelations of otter, urchin, kelp, and fishes. The otter's role in the structuring and regulation of various communities within the marine ecosystem is only beginning to be recognized and documented."

DR. JOHN S. PEARSE conducted a seminar on sea otters at the University of California at Santa Cruz, in which Judson Vandevere, Dan Miller, Dr. Betty Davis, and others participated, including fishermen and conservationists. Upon conclusion of the sessions, Dr. Betty Davis summarized its findings as follows: "The southern sea otter is beginning to reoccupy areas where it existed at least a million years before humans arrived along the California shoreline. Along with this gradual reoccupation of its former range, the otter is feeding upon large numbers of marine invertebrates of various kinds within kelp forests. It is not endangering the survival of any invertebrate species, but rather is limiting the numbers and sizes of certain kinds, while enhancing the growth and numbers of others. . . .

"The otter's profound effects on productivity and on the structures and dynamic relationships within kelp communities are obviously very complex and incompletely understood. Only an inkling of their intricacies has been hinted at in the few studies thus far. Such investigations have indicated, however, that as a result of preying on grazers—such as sea urchins, abalones, kelp crabs, and snails—sea otters enhance primary reproduction of benthic algae in kelp forests. Such enhancement leads to particularly rich and diverse kelp forests in terms of the species diversity of biota present. Species diversity is generally regarded as a prime requisite for a healthy and stable ecosystem."

"And, from the Aleutian Islands to the north come similar indications of a strong correlation among otters, urchins, and kelp and of the enhancement effects of otters. . . . The otters effectively control sea urchin populations and the absence of grazing pressure allows vegetational communities to flourish. Conversely, reducing the population of sea otters makes it possible for the urchin population to increase and this leads to a significant reduction in the size of the kelp beds and associated communities. . . .

"We feel a detailed assessment of the sea otters' role, in all its parameters, is needed before decisions about range restrictions can be made intelligently."

SOME YEARS AGO, at the invitation of George S. Lockwood, president of the Monterey Kelp Corp., I went out early one morning on one of the company's kelp cutters, which was operating that day in Carmel Bay. Present also were Dan Miller of the DFG and Jud Vandevere of the FSO. Dan and an assistant were checking the crabs, snails, and other small marine life being swept up in the rotating cutters of the boat as the kelp was brought up on a beltlike apparatus and then dumped into the hold. Jud was on hand to see that the operation posed no hazards to sea otters. I was there to take pictures and obtain background material for a feature which ran in the *Weekend Magazine* section of the *Monterey Peninsula Herald*.

The surface of the bay was also dotted with several canoes and kayaks being paddled by some dedicated young members of Ventana chapter of the Sierra Club, who had been informed that otter pups might get trapped in the kelp as it was being harvested.

Though the skipper of the cutter was keeping a sharp eye from the bridge to see that no otters were in danger, it appeared to most of the rest of us that the otters were too smart to get near the cutter, whose engines made enough underwater noise to warn them off. On other occasions the FSO asked small-boat owners not to feed the otters lest they become too trusting and swim into the cutting blades of propellers. But in this case no otter came within 75 yards of the boat.

Recognizing the fact that the otters devour the urchins that destroy his company's principal resource—kelp—Lockwood was as anxious as anyone to protect them. For kelp yields that "magic" all-purpose substance, algin, used as a water control compound, stabilizer, and emulsifier in everything from ice cream to beer to pharmaceuticals to paint to oil-well drilling, in which it substitutes for mud as a drill lubricant.

FOR THOSE PEOPLE who fear that they will have to forego eating abalones if the otters are to survive, Lockwood has a word of encouragement. He is also president-founder of Monterey Abalone Farms, which raises this now-gourmet item onshore in a former warehouse on Cannery Row. He and his partner, Dr. Fred T. Schulz, consulting geneticist and biometrician, after seven years of intensive research and experimentation have successfully raised abalones from spawn to three-inch size and at this writing were seeking an expansion site in order to grow them to commercial size and begin supplying an ever-growing world market. They expected to harvest their first crop in two years.

There was a time when Lockwood had his own pet otter—named George—which showed up every afternoon at about 5 o'clock in the Monterey Bay water behind the abalone farm. Some inferior breeding stock had occasionally been tossed to George, who was not about to miss a handout. But as techniques were perfected at the plant, the handouts became fewer, and George finally took off for greener pastures.

California Marine Associates of Cayucos has also been pioneering abalone hatching and growing for the past 10 years with good success. They are working with a major oil company, ARCO, to grow hatchery-raised abalones on offshore oil-drilling platforms in the Santa Barbara Channel.

Meanwhile, Nate Shafer and his Pacific Ocean Farms are planting hatchery-raised red abalones in special chambers anchored offshore in Monterey Bay. And Dick Hirschkind has a five-acre lease on three experimental habitats to determine if it is feasible to grow abalones there.

All work closely together through the California Aquaculture Association. So it looks as if, in the foreseeable future, there may be commercial raising of abalones. At present, however, problems arise when the abalones reach about 3 inches. These may not be legally salable in the U.S., but they are in Japan and could bring surprisingly high prices there—prices Americans would not now pay for 3-inch abalones. So for the near future, at least, commercially raised abalones may go mostly to Japan and to Hong Kong markets. Mr. Lockwood, one notices, in discussing the future of his company, speaks of a world market, rather than a California market.

Mature adult abalone, lifted out of the seawater tank in which it was feeding on brown algae, displays the large muscular foot from which abalone "steaks" are sliced. Mature adults emit eggs or sperms into the seawater through the openings in the shell—sperms in little puffs or eggs singly. Monterey Abalone Farms. (R. Buchsbaum)

Young abalones, about half-an-inch in length, raised at Monterey Abalone Farms, Monterey, California. The California Department of Fish and Game is buying large numbers of these juvenile forms, which will be planted in nearshore waters in the attempt to increase the declining abalone population. (R. Buchsbaum)

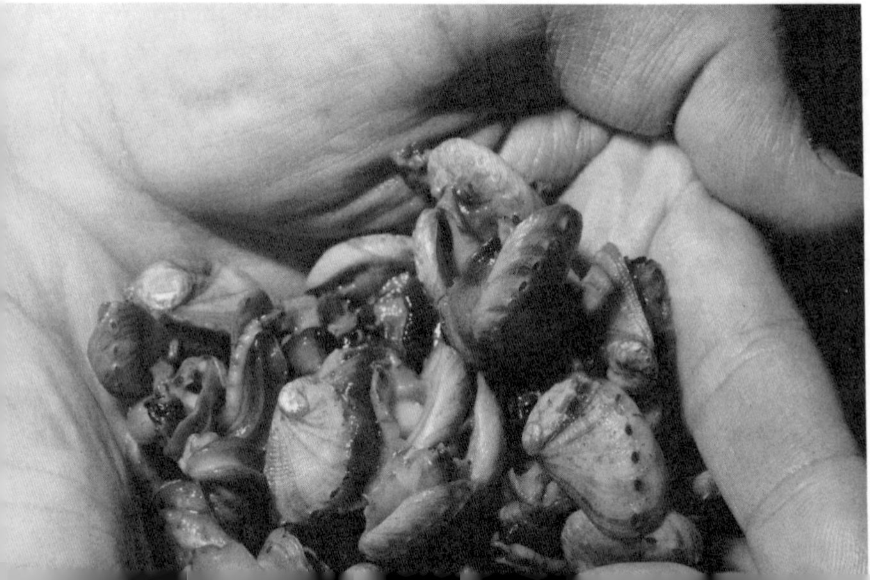

10

THE CONTROVERSY CONTINUES

WITH the inauguration of oil tanker traffic from Alaska, the FSO became increasingly concerned with the threat of spills within the otters' range. Fifty thousand DWT tankers moor and offload at each end of the range, with 90,000-130,000 DWT tanker mooring terminal facilities planned for one of these sites in the future.

As aforementioned, oil-coating of an otter's pelage would be fatal since its body warmth depends upon the integrity of its fur.

The FSO has been disturbed also about the lack of a sufficient DFG warden force to "curtail ruthless shooting, bludgeoning, netting, and ramming with boats by those who view otters as competitors for shellfish and a threat to their livelihood or sport pleasures."

THUS THE FSO sought "endangered" status for the otters under the federal Endangered Species Act. Since 1972 they had been guarded under the Marine Mammal Protection Act, a logical culmination to the protection which has slowly increased since an international moratorium on the killing of sea otters was established in 1911 under the terms of an International Fur Seal Treaty.

In 1913 California adopted a law that prohibited the taking or possession of sea otters for their pelts, though at the time there was little evidence that any otters remained to protect. About 30 were spotted off Santa Catalina Island in 1916 and a few more had taken refuge along the rugged Big Sur coastline. Dr. Carl E. Hubbs, Professor of Biology Emeritus, Scripps Institution of

Oceanography, wrote to the *Otter Raft,* publication of Friends of the Sea Otter: "I had the rare privilege of having seen an adult sea otter scampering over the intertidal kelp at Gorda in 1916, when I carried out a survey of the inshore fish fauna along the central California coast. Years ago, I saw one on a Coast Guard flight around San Miguel Island and my technician, Al Allanson, saw one later on a trip to San Miguel."

Hans Ewoldsen, a pioneer resident of Big Sur, has told of his first personal acquaintance with otters in the fall of 1929:

"My wife's father, John Pfeiffer, several neighbors, and I were fishing from a small boat in the kelp beds south of Point Sur. Mr. Pfeiffer pointed out to us several animal heads showing above the water and told us they were sea otters. If we had noticed them before he pointed them out to us, we had probably taken them for seal or kelp heads. He warned us not to tell outsiders about seeing the sea otters since they were supposed to be extinct. He did this not because he had any plans to harm them, but on the contrary, he wanted to protect them. That the existence of the sea otters here was unknown is not strange since this part of the coast was isolated and not much visited by people who might recognize a sea otter."

When the coast road, Highway 1, was extended through Big Sur in 1938, it opened up the Bixby Creek area where most of the remnant otter population lived. Thus the general public learned that the otters had not been completely wiped out in California. In 1941 a sea otter refuge was established for the otters from Malpaso Creek to Dolan Creek, and in 1957 the area was increased from the Carmel River mouth in Monterey County to Santa Rosa Creek in San Luis Obispo County.

Between 1916 and 1939 the abalone industry had landed in excess of 41 million pounds of abalone along the Monterey County coast. When construction of the highway was completed in 1939, it was noticed that cuts, fills, and slides, which had dumped large amounts of rocks and soil into the ocean, had changed the abalone habitat, which had suffered considerably from siltation. Areas near Mill Creek, Rockland Landing, Plaskett Creek, and Cape San Martin had been altered by the road work, with the result that abalones could no longer be found there by the commercial fishermen who began moving their operations farther south.

According to the DFG, the "raft" which had been discovered in 1938 by the Howard Sharpes had apparently ranged between Pfeiffer Point and Point Sur during the early 1900s. Hans Ewoldsen had described them as "acting like animals which migrate in herds to a new feeding ground."

In a report based largely on evidence presented by abalone divers, the DFG stated that "by March 1938 the otter range had moved up to Bixby Creek, and to Notley's Landing by July 1938 ... The migrant front was at Malpaso Creek in 1947, Yankee Point in 1951-52, the south shore of Point Lobos in 1954, Carmel Bay in 1956, Cypress Point in 1959, and Monterey Bay in 1963.

"To the south, they were into the Gorda area in 1950. There were hearsay reports of 100 being killed near Pt. Piedras Blancas. For several years the sea otters remained just north of San Simeon Point, until December 1965, when 65 moved into the Pico Creek area." Margaret Owings reports having lived at Gibson Beach, the southern end of Point Lobos, and having watched Disney Studios make their first sea otter film there in the offshore waters during the 1949-50 period.

In 1965 commercial abalone fishermen, primarily from Morro Bay, who had harvested 1,776,540 pounds of abalones, the largest ever recorded, returned to their fishing grounds to find their resources dwindling. They placed the blame on foraging sea otters. They persuaded State Senator Donald L. Grunsky in 1970 to introduce Senate Bill 442 to give the State Department of Fish and Game the authority to manage sea otters outside their otter refuge. The FSO, not unmindful that fish and shellfish catches were dropping catastrophically around the world, sent a delegation to Sacramento, and their arguments were apparently convincing. The bill was defeated.

"Who ate all these abalones?" is a question easily answered. The 1965 commercial abalone harvest at Morro Bay piled up all these shells, and many more. No animal as slow-growing as the abalone can stand this kind of pressure indefinitely. (J.A. Mattison, Jr.)

IN JULY 1968 Paul Wild and Jack Ames of the DFG began a five-year study to investigate this problem, but in 1972 the federal Marine Mammal Protection Act precluded the state of California from implementing an otter management program unless it would protect the otter and its ecosystem or qualify as scientific research. A program, already being drawn up, was nevertheless presented to the Marine Mammal Commission by the DFG in 1974, but was returned for more data on the biology and dynamics of the sea otter and its environment. It had been hotly protested by FSO and the California chapters of the Sierra Club.

In October 1975 the DFG completed a revised and larger management program, *A Proposal for Sea Otter Protection and for the Return of Management to the State of California*. It requested a waiver of the moratorium on "taking" of animals, and a return of management to the state.

THIS NEW PROPOSAL was submitted to the U.S. Fish and Wildlife Service in January 1976. It provided for a research program of from 8 to 10 years, covering a 230-mile linear coastline distance from Miramontes Point in San Mateo County to Avila in San Luis Obispo County. Subsequently arrangements were made with the University of California at Santa Barbara and the Moss Landing Marine Laboratories of the California State Colleges to undertake research to determine the effects of otter foraging of certain marine organisms. With this knowledge of sea otter impact on the marine environment and the feasibility of "zonation and translocation as a management tool," the DFG would be able to assess management alternatives, it was stated.

WHEN, in January 1977 the U.S. Fish and Wildlife Service listed the southern sea otter of the central California coast as a "threatened " species, the Friends of the Sea Otter hailed the action as a milestone and as proof of national recognition for the organization's efforts, but sent out a cautionary message signed by Margaret Owings to its membership:

"Certainly, we are not happy that our sea otters are 'threatened' but we are grateful for this designation which lays the foundation for protective measures that the otters need as well as official concern for their critical habitat. Under the Endangered Species Act (of 1973), otters can't be touched without a research permit from the Marine Mammal Commission. We are grateful for the protection afforded by the Commission, with their judgments on an issue that could not otherwise have become disentangled from the local market catch of shellfish and its soaring prices. We hope that this 'threatened' status will cause the State to reassess its position as to habitat and management of the California sea otter and we look to Governor Brown and his enlightened attitude towards marine mammals, to realign and set a new policy for the State at an early date."

WITHIN A SHORT TIME, the FSO found cause to send its membership an "action alert," using Shakespeare's famous words spoken by Henry V at Agincourt: "Once more into the breach, dear Friends, once more!" It continued: "A notice of the revised two-year California Fish and Game 'research permit' request to capture, tag, and translocate otters appeared in the *Federal Register*—triggering the need for immediate action. ...

"The permit, if approved, would set the stage for restricting the southern range of otters at Point San Luis and translocating them to an unspecified site near Santa Cruz to the north. It would begin the containment of all otters within a 230-mile coastal stretch to protect shellfisheries. ..."

In August 1977 the DFG obtained a permit for a single translocation of 40 otters to the waters off Sand Hill Bluff, north of Santa Cruz. The FSO approves of this project, but as of February 1979 no attempt has been made by the DFG to carry out this translocation of sea otters.

Originally the FSO favored San Nicolas Island (west of Santa Catalina Island and the most distant of the Channel Islands) as the site for otter translocation. Its distance from the mainland, its rough waters, and restrictions imposed by the Navy, discourage and limit abalone divers. There are kelp beds and abundant otter food, and otters once thrived there, but when the island was proposed as an LNG (liquid natural gas) site, the FSO lost interest in San Nicolas. Now that the proposal to establish an LNG site at the island has been canceled, the FSO again looks at San Nicolas Island as its first choice for the establishment of an otter colony isolated from the main coastal population, which lies between two oil-tanker ports.

The state has opposed any transfer of otters to the offshore islands, the DFG stating that these islands are presently the backbone of the remaining commercial abalone and spiny lobster fisheries in California. Both San Miguel and San Nicolas, which had been previously considered, have thus been dropped as possible translocation sites, along with the other islands in the Santa Barbara Channel. San Miguel has recently been declared a "Marine Mammal Reserve" by the federal government. Anacapa and Santa Barbara Islands have been made national monuments but their waters have been transferred from federal jurisdiction to that of the California DFG, which promptly granted kelp-cutting contracts.

When Dr. Robert C. Stebbins, professor of zoology, University of California, Berkeley, wrote to the U.S. Fish and Wildlife Service in Washington, D.C., urging classification of the Pacific sea otter as at least "rare" and the southern population as "endangered," he made the point that "we should not allow current signs of species expansion to lead to complacency. Recent studies of littoral and sublittoral marine communities have shown the otter to be an important element in long-term productivity in such environments. We must not allow emotional reactions to declining fisheries (the causes of which cannot be blamed on the otter) to sway our actions.

"The return of the sea otter to its former habitats seems clearly, on scientific grounds, to be in the best interests of ecological integrity of Pacific coastal waters."

SELDOM, if ever, has any other small animal, friendly and captivating and numbering fewer than 2,000 in all, been the center of a running battle between a citizens' conservation group and a state governmental agency also charged with insuring its continued preservation.

Shore waters in which otters thrive are likely to prove best for the humans who live along that shore. (J.A. Mattison, Jr.)

11

A COMPROMISE OF SORTS

AFTER AT LEAST SEVEN YEARS of controversy between the Friends of the Sea Otter and the California Department of Fish and Game over the advisability and feasibility of restricting the southern sea otters' range, trying to translocate frontal animals that stray out of the range, and concern over the need to establish new breeding populations elsewhere along the Pacific Coast, an agreement was finally reached in July 1977.

In May 1977 President Jimmy Carter, in his Environmental Program, directed heads of federal departments and agencies to provide information on critical habitat for endangered and threatened species, including the southern sea otter. Under the Endangered Species Act of 1973, critical habitat is identified as the area of land, water, and airspace required for the normal needs and survival of a species. These needs include space for growth, movement, and normal behavior; food and water; sites for breeding and rearing of young; cover or shelter; and various other biological, physical, and economic requirements.

Before critical habitat is determined, biological data are obtained and analyzed, and federal and state agencies are contacted in writing prior to publication of a proposal. Written comments on that proposal are then sought from all interested parties and public hearings may be held. The FSO reported that it would be "gathering pertinent information on those factors critical for survival and recovery of the southern sea otter in the months to come."

MEANWHILE it had reached a compromise with Director Charles Fullerton of the DFG on the final version of a research permit application submitted to the U.S. Fish and Wildlife Service, and revised several times since its original submission in 1976.

"The agreements reached," said Betty Davis in *The Otter Raft,* "should be beneficial to all concerned, including the otters, since they will lay the necessary groundwork for future trans-locations of a viable population to well-removed reserve breeding sites, away from the high oil-spill potential of their present distribution."

THE DFG in its 1977 revision requested permission to:

1. Capture and tag young otters throughout the range over a two-year period to determine their distribution, movements, and mortality rate.

2. Capture and tag for observation animals in the northern "front" group nearing Santa Cruz.

3. Capture, tag, and move 40 otters (30 male, 10 female) taken from four different sections of the range over a one-year period. These otters would be translocated to a site on the coast somewhere north of Santa Cruz, "beyond the present front group." At the end of the year there would be a federal and public review to determine whether further experimentation of this sort was necessary.

The FSO objected to a preliminary version of this final revision that would have repeated the translocation of another 40 the second year of study, making 80 in all "with open-ended number of actual captures necessary to accomplish this." It was agreed in further meetings with Fullerton that the first experiment would involve only 12 animals from the southern front, rather than the 20 proposed. At the end of the first year the FSO and DFG were to meet again to decide whether there was any need for more translocation experimentation.

The FSO strongly urged that translocation sites in California be considered before sites in Oregon and Washington, as proposed by the DFG, be examined. Fullerton agreed that the north coast of California was probably richer in food and refuge areas than the coasts farther north. The DFG had also included British Columbia and Alaska as possible translocation sites, and have not removed these from consideration despite strong objections from the FSO.

"Otters will be captured by using the diver-held underwater capture device designed and successfully used by the California Department of Fish and Game," the permit application stated. "However, when conditions warrant, we propose to use a tangle net (9-inch stretch net, 20 feet deep, 300 feet long) which will be monitored at all times. This method has been used recently by Ancel M. Johnson in Prince William Sound to capture 16 sea otters with no mortalities. By using a tangle net we can capture otters more effectively when conditions such as poor underwater visibility preclude using the special diver-held device." (See p. 131.)

The DFG has stated that "although every effort will be made to eliminate accidental mortality it is unrealistic to expect that there will be no deaths. We expect that, even with great care, accidental mortality may reach 10 percent."

All animals moved were to be double tagged on the hind flippers with a plastic tag for ready identification. Once at their new site, they were to be maintained in large ocean holding pens for periods varying from one to eight days before release, in hopes of diminishing their homing instincts and avoiding quick dispersal. "Such tests are necessary," said Betty Davis, "to assure a successful eventual translocation of otters to a reserve colony, with a minimum of loss due to mortality or dispersal. It will permit the DFG to develop and refine capture, transportation, and holding methodology. ... Transportation will be in water-filled pens by boat or refrigerated vans."

IN AN EARLIER translocation experiment in 1969 when the DFG tried to move otters out of commercial abalone beds and back into the "refuge," one observer remarked that "it was just like trying to pour more water into a full glass. The otters just 'ran over' and spilled from the refuge again."

However, Karl Kenyon has reported the successful transfer of 62 otters from Amchitka by air to the Quillayute, Washington, airstrip in July 1970 for release off the Washington and Oregon coasts. Their cages were moved onto truck beds cooled by layers of cracked ice. "Some animals whistled softly; others remained silent and completely calm," Kenyon recalled in an article for *National Geographic.* "A good sign, I thought; they're going to make it. And they did make it." But not for long. By 1977 very few could be found (see page 135).

IN THE FINAL VERSION of its 1977 application the DFG decided not to attempt to restrict the otters' southern dispersal movement, at least for the time being. Any frontal animals emigrating south from Avila were to be let alone. The study for establishing new populations was to be done in cooperation with the Department of the Interior (Fish and Wildlife Service) and National Marine Fisheries Service, with the FWS assuming the responsibility for the segment of the study outside California.

Once the sites and their potential carrying capacity were determined, the agencies involved were to come up with a working agreement on the jurisdiction and funding "for protection of the population from adverse human impact"; they were to allocate federal funds for mitigation of loss of shellfish resources; and the FWS and Marine Mammal Commission were to be asked to formulate the legal requirements and approve a management program to maintain the population.

That word "maintain" was important to the FSO, for it had originally been spelled "contain," which connoted the same old policy of trying to restrict the otters to a limited range. Director Fullerton himself, however, suggested the change in wording. "We were immensely gratified to see this change in attitude," commented Betty Davis.

"The Friends of the Sea Otter advisory committee feels that this two-year proposal is acceptable and should produce the information needed before attempting a larger translocation," the official FSO statement read. "It should also indicate the feasibility of any future management plan based on translocating otters." (See also page 117.)

THERE ARE possibly 200 different combinations of color, shape, and placement that can be used in the tagging of otters for identification so that each individual animal can be known to the investigator. Earl Ebert planned to use them all when he inherited the DFG's otter program from Dan Miller in the fall of 1977.

Miller had been transferred to the kelp-sea urchin management program, and Ebert, superintendent of operations at the DFG's laboratory at Granite Canyon south of Carmel, had the otter program added to his other duties.

Sea otters were nothing new to Ebert, who had been with the department for some 20 years and began otter studies in 1966. But more recently he had been primarily concerned with aquaculture and mariculture. When I talked to him in October 1977, he confessed to being a little overwhelmed by having to take the additional assignment, but already had his program organized and under way. Just the preceding week he had received a permit from the U.S. Fish and Wildlife Service to tag 200 otters, 100 per year for two years, and almost at once had 35 animals with the small identifying plastics clipped into the webbing of a hind flipper.

"The emphasis now is on research," he said as he looked out of the window of his laboratory office at the ocean beyond. "We've got to get away from a polarized stance and have people at work who are very objective. I've seen too many battles. We've been laboring too many years to find a scapegoat for the disappearance of the shellfish fisheries—otters, skindivers, commercial fishermen, sports fishermen.

"The abalone fishery out of Morro Bay has been one of the most colorful operations in the world, probably second only to the women pearl divers of Japan. I would hate to see it vanish.

"Of course I also believe that abalone could be farmed along this shoreline better than anywhere else in the world. A realistic scheme would be for certain sections of the nearshore environment to be set aside for shellfish farming, and other sections for parks. Meanwhile, we do have an otter research project to carry out."

The censusing of otters will continue, probably every other year, Ebert said. "Dan Miller set up a good system, with about 30 shoreline observers and a plane for the aerial survey. He feels that a biennial check is sufficient along the approximately 175-mile otter range."

A concerted study was set up by the DFG in the 8 to 10-mile stretch between San Simeon and the Cambria radar station to determine its carrying capacity—how many otters it could support. With Ebert as administrator, three other DFG biologists were pulled in from other projects and assigned to the new program: Bob Hardy heading field investigations out of Morro Bay, with Fred Wendell as assistant, and Jack Ames reporting from Monterey. All three are divers.

"We had to make a concentrated effort in a small area," said Ebert. "We're seeking additional seasonal help from Cal Poly at San Luis Obispo—students with spotting scopes, binoculars, etc.

"Next year we plan to translocate some animals from the Cambria-Pt. Buchon area to an area just north of Santa Cruz, near Natural Bridges State Park—Sand Hill Bluff. In conjunction with Moss Landing Marine Laboratories we've been studying the biota there—the ecosystem—so that we know what is on hand before the otters come in. There will have been a full year of this study prior to their arrival." (Such a transfer of otters has not been made by February 1979, as mentioned earlier.)

A periodic and frequent beach walk of all study areas, and complete necropsies of all animals found dead, is part of the study program, as are continued conferences with such experts as Dr. Victor Morejohn at Moss Landing, veterinarian Dr. Thomas Williams, Judson Vandevere, Dr. James Mattison, etc., Ebert emphasized.

"Biologists are notorious for their inability to communicate

Captive sea otter, netted near Cambria, California, is released from transport cage at Big Creek, California, by Fish and Game personnel. (J.A. Mattison, Jr.)

their entire aim and purpose and feelings," he remarked wryly. "I've been in Sacramento at legislative meetings and done my best as a biologist to present facts, only to get the feeling that I was talking to a brick wall. So an integral part of this new program is to work with as many knowledgeable people as possible.

"We don't want to alienate anyone unnecessarily, but I know that we're in a very controversial situation and I doubt whether we can please both sides."

Earl Ebert agrees with Dan Miller that "you can't have unlimited shellfish fisheries and unlimited otters." But Keith Cox of the DFG said this even before Miller did, Ebert points out, "and I became convinced of it when I took over the abalone investigative program more than 10 years ago. We now have 175 miles of sea otters and 175 miles of no shellfish fisheries. I've seen the recreational fisheries of Pismo clams disappear at Monterey Bay and being threatened at Pismo Beach.

"When otters were hunted and removed from the scene, abalones, urchins, and other shellfish flourished. An artificial situation developed. Man took advantage of this imbalance to increase his tonnage of shellfish taken. The fisheries that developed in the absence of the otter were really artificial. Now we have some very tough and objective decisions to make.

"Man removed the top predator from a food chain and created a disclimax. Then man took advantage of this disclimax to build up his fisheries. You have to believe that this is one of the all-time classics in terms of what man can do to disrupt a situation.

"Our stance at this point is one of research. I think we've learned some very good lessons and that we're getting better at doing our homework. Personally I think that the sea otter is the most interesting animal esthetically in the world."

Assuming that the sea otter population is allowed to increase in a normal fashion and that its range expands at the current rate of two to three miles per year in each direction—north and south—Ebert foresees an increase in mortalities, "since this is an animal very vulnerable to men and boats and human activity." He categorizes oil spills, however, along with lightning strikes and the fall of meteorites, and refuses to join "the doomsday projectors who see a potential spill in every tanker."

At Scripps Institution, he reported, the effects of different types and weights of oil were being tested on otter pelages, along with means for getting rid of the oil.

As for the future of abalones, sea urchins, crabs, and other shellfish, "we'll always have them," he predicted, "though at present as they emerge from the rock crevices, the sea otters get them. Man should be able to achieve a normal balance again, and eventually he will."

Ebert's optimism is not shared by the biologists on the Advisory Committee of the FSO. They take more seriously the common-sense approach of the abalone fishermen's cooperative of Enseñada, Baja California, who in August 1978 voted to reduce their catch by one-third. At Enseñada there are no sea otters, and the fishermen know very well who has been getting the abalones.

12

KEEPING TAB ON OTTERS

SINCE 1974 John and Vicki Pearse, and in their absences John's undergraduate students at U.C. Santa Cruz, have been systematically recording the sea otters seen off West Cliff Drive in the city of Santa Cruz, along a distance of three miles. Visits of about 30 minutes each are made almost every day and the kelp canopies and surrounding waters are searched with binoculars for the presence of sea otters at this northern fringe of the main sea otter range. On many of these visits the Pearses took with them their 2-year-old son Devon, and the observations that were verbalized were not entirely lost on him. Whenever he had access to windows that directly overlooked Monterey Bay kelp beds, he picked up any convenient cylindrical object, put it to his eye, and solemnly intoned "no otters."

Nevertheless, in the 36 months from 1974 through 1976 the Pearses did record an average of one otter every other day. Most of the sightings were of single animals, and the maximum sighting for the entire period was a total of six animals, distributed at three different sites, on 30 November 1976. In March 1977 about 50 sea otters moved into the kelp forests at Soquel Point, not far southeast of Santa Cruz, and in the spring of 1978 the number had stabilized at about 40 animals.

Expansion of the range of sea otters has been warmly greeted, as a measure of their success, by the Friends of the Sea Otter. But at Princeton, in a sports diving area on the San Mateo coast north of Santa Cruz County, "the otters are coming" has become a rallying cry. At a meeting of skin divers addressed by a member of the DFG, who did little in his talk to discourage such fears, one aroused listener threatened to go out and shoot sea otters. The startled DFG speaker had to urge him to use more subtle means for protecting the supply of abalones from otters.

The divers, as well as the otters and their friends, may soon have new concerns. As early as 1971, Pacific Gas and Electric Company engaged Cayot and North to prepare an Environmental Impact Report in expectation of installing a nuclear power plant at Davenport, north of Santa Cruz. Davenport is about midway between Santa Cruz Point and Año Nuevo Island, a distance of about 24 miles along the coast of Santa Cruz and San Mateo counties. This stretch of coast is also looked on favorably by companies preparing applications for oil-drilling sites.

In anticipation of the arrival of the sea otters, nuclear plants, and oil rigs, the DFG and also the university biologists at the marine laboratories at UC Santa Cruz and at Moss Landing have been making studies of this coastal area and its resources of kelps, of fishes, and of the invertebrates in the kelp forests and the intertidal shore areas.

In 1977 Yellin, Agegian, and Pearse published a report titled "Ecological Benchmarks in the Santa Cruz County Kelp Forests Before the Reestablishment of Sea Otters." They concluded that the area surveyed, from Point Santa Cruz north to Año Nuevo Island, is suitable for supporting populations of sea otters "which will almost certainly be established along the coast in the near future." They observed that the Point Santa Cruz area, the southern extreme of the study area, is not necessarily "typical" because it is not far from a sewer outfall and "has been a popular diving spot for decades; abalones are scarce and human impact has probably been significant." There is also "a significant amount of impact from both commercial and sport fishermen" along most of the study area. The only good abalone beds are the ones almost inaccessible to human divers—those just north of Scott Creek and at Año Nuevo Island. At Año Nuevo both otters and divers would be at high risk from the sharks attracted there by large numbers of elephant seals and other sea mammals.

Sea urchin beds, however, are another matter; in the absence of otters, sea urchins flourish. The survey showed good beds of big red urchins to the seaward side of the *Macrocystis* kelp beds, and also occasional large beds of the smaller purple urchins on the landward side. In 1976 sea urchin beds at Point Santa Cruz and at Año Nuevo were decimated by a disease that first became visible when spines began to fall off the animals. Diseased urchins in small numbers are still seen all along the coast of Santa Cruz

Diseased sea urchins collected near Santa Cruz. (J.S. Pearse)

County. This serves to remind researchers that feeding relationships are not the only factors involved in the ups and downs of animal populations, whether sea urchins, abalones, otters, or crabs. The San Francisco Bay area, that once supported a great commercial crab fishery, no longer does so. Pollution is probably a factor, but so also may be a nemertean worm that is found in the egg masses of crabs. No one can blame the otters, who are still dawdling at Soquel Point more than 125 miles to the south.

Aerial surveys made by the DFG between May 1970 and June 1976 have recorded all the otters sighted during each flight at locations along the 24-mile stretch from Point Santa Cruz (the northern limit of Monterey Bay) to Año Nuevo. Counting otters from the ground or from the air is one way of keeping tab on them but it answers only a limited number of questions. To trace the dispersion of otters from an established area, to know how far they migrate, which ones return to the established area, whether they are males or females, or whether territorial or non-territorial males—in other words, to follow their movements and come to understand what is happening to the otter population—otters must be recognized as individuals.

TO DO THAT biologists of the DFG and at the universities obtain permits from the Marine Mammal Commission to capture and tag otters or attach radio transmitters.

Tags are usually plastic, color-coded and numbered, and placed at distinctive sites in the webbing between toes. Keeping in touch with an otter day or night, however, requires telemetry. A miniature radio transmitter is attached to a collar placed around the neck or to a tag placed on the flipper.

Attaching the transmitter to a flipper tag is the easiest and safest method, but it is useful only for determining the *location* of an otter that is being observed over a period of time. The whip antenna of the transmitter is vertical, and in a rafting otter it protrudes out of the water, so that the signal can be detected at a much greater distance than that of the horizontally oriented antenna attached to a collar. Unfortunately, the collar method is the only one that can yield information about feeding bouts, resting periods, or other specific behaviors. To keep track of these, it is necessary to risk possible injury to the animal from lacerations of the neck by the collar—and also injury to the experimenter who must subdue the animal with nets and physical force in order to attach the collar. Dr. Tom Williams has successfully used an anesthetic to prepare otters for the

Capturing and tagging. This is the net device used by the California Department of Fish and Game for capturing sea otters. The diver approaches the animal from underneath and then pulls the drawstring to close the net around the animal. (J.A. Mattison, Jr.)

Diver pushes device toward boat.
(DFG)

Net and animal are hauled aboard.
(DFG)

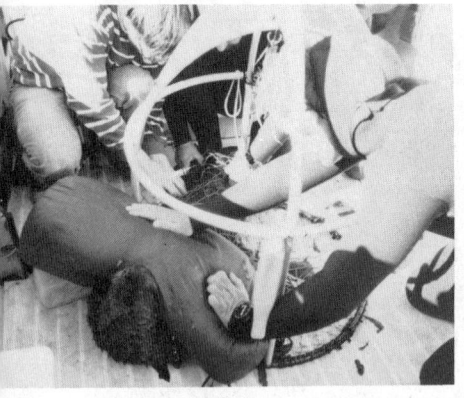

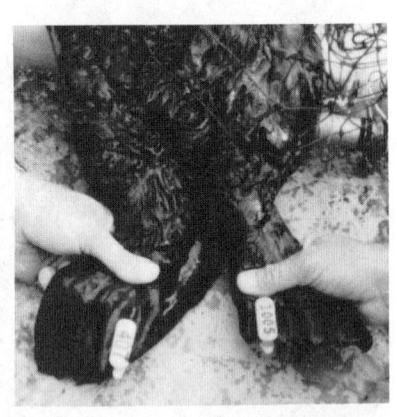

Pillow is held across otter while
tags are attached. (DFG)

Plastic identification tags have
been fastened to hind flippers. (DFG)

Sea otter in a tangle-net, a device used to capture otters for experimental studies or translocation. Prince William Sound, Alaska. (Daniel Costa)

Experimental soiling of a sea otter with crude oil at Prince William Sound, Alaska. Ancel Johnson, *left,* is applying the oil. Dr. Tom Williams, *right,* is taking the otter's rectal temperature in an attempt to check the degree of stress suffered by the otter. (D. Costa)

attachment of a collar, and this is not only easier on the experimenter but assures a better fit of the collar.

The click rate of the transmitter responds to temperature changes, and Thomas Loughlin found that the click rate of a collar transmitter is low when the animal is feeding and the transmitter is repeatedly immersed. As the otter starts to groom, however, the transmitter under the chin is out of the water and is warmed by the high surface temperature of an otter that has just finished a strenuous feeding bout. As the otter continues to ruffle its fur in feeding, the animal cools off and the click rate of the transmitter slows.

KEEPING TRACK of transplanted otters has been the special interest of Ron Jameson, who wrote his thesis on the translocation of otter populations when he took his M.S. degree at Oregon State University. As research biologist for the U.S. Fish and Wildlife Service, he has probably covered more Pacific Coast territory, from Prince William Sound, Alaska, to southern San Luis Obispo County, California, than any other sea otter investigator.

When this was written, Ancel Johnson, Jameson's immediate superior, was headquartered at Anchorage, Alaska. Ron himself was occupying office space with the California Department of Fish and Game in Monterey, but was expecting to be moved in the near future to the Piedras Blancas Light Station in San Luis Obispo County, which the FWS had bid for after the Coast Guard had automated its operation there, leaving the property available along with sizeable laboratory space and living quarters.

"To speed up the range expansion and establish new areas, the first attempt at translocation was made by Karl Kenyon in Alaska in 1955," he said. "The animals succumbed to soiled fur and exposure and the experiment failed. Ten years later Alaska tried again, moving the animals from Amchitka Island in the Aleutians to escape the proposed nuclear test. Most were taken to southeast Alaska. Later, between 1969 and 1972, others were taken to British Columbia, Washington, and Oregon. "Over a four-year period, southeast Alaska received 403. In 1975, six years after the last of the transplants, a month's investigation aboard a vessel cruising the area turned up 479, including pups. Obviously, this translocation attempt looked like a success.

"This year [1977] biologist Ian MacKaskie reported from British Columbia that of 89 removed there, 60 could still be found, off Vancouver Island. In Washington, I could find only 18 of 59 released off the outer coastline of the Olympic Peninsula, and in Oregon, only four out of 93. Karl Kenyon, though retired now, comes out whenever he is needed, and has worked with me the past two years on this monitoring.

"Since none of these transplanted animals was ever tagged, who is to know whether some of the Washington and Oregon populations moved up to British Columbia? My best count ever in Oregon was 23, including pups. This shrank to 13, then 12, now four."

Jameson says that he has seen no indication of any of the translocated animals moving south. All observations of movement have shown them traveling north. "As a scientist I can't say that this is a definite trend, since they were not marked," he observed. "But I have a feeling that this is what has been happening.

"There can be very rapid declines in population. At one translocation site, seven animals were found dead in the first few days. Due to infrequent pupping by females, ... deaths frequently outnumber births. And males may move away, searching for other females in estrus.

"I think that now, however, we can accomplish translocations with little if any mortality, having vastly improved our techniques."

The purpose of the Endangered Species Act, Jameson states, is "to get the animals off the threatened and endangered list. And the Fish and Wildlife Service has the responsibility for accomplishing this. So we've been looking at possible new habitats for at least some of the California sea otters, which are all threatened primarily because they're restricted to a small range and can be the victims of oil spills."

Once established at Piedras Blancas, Jameson plans to begin marking animals and following their activity patterns. "Not enough is known on their detailed behavior," he said. "Are they territorial, males or females? Is information accurate on their reproductive cycle? How does the otter influence its environment, and vice versa? We may end up being the good guys or the villains in the eyes of the public, in this matter of translocation, but we hope in a couple of years to know much more about the otters' behavior and social structure."

Tags attached to hind flippers are made of plastic, and are color coded and numbered, and attached at specific locations in the webbing of each foot. Sometimes the observer may have to watch a single otter for hours before it displays the flippers in a position in which the numbers can be read. (R. Buchsbaum)

13

THE OTTERS GO TO COLLEGE

THOUGH DETAILED RESEARCH on the southern sea otter did not start until the late 1960s, few sea mammals have enjoyed such academic attention since that time. There's scarcely an institution of higher learning up and down the California coast from Berkeley to La Jolla, that doesn't have some otter research project under way yielding material for theses or pamphlets, some of them funded by federal Sea Grant money for the benefit of the Fish and Wildlife Service and the California Department of Fish and Game; in addition to which the DFG has its own projects and publications which keep a number of specialists employed.

Eventually all this material may be combined into one treatise. Meanwhile, the University of California Berkeley, UC Santa Cruz, Moss Landing Marine Laboratories of the California State Colleges, Stanford Research Institute, Hopkins Marine Station, California Polytechnic Institute at San Luis Obispo, UC Santa Barbara, Santa Barbara Natural History Museum, UCLA, and Scripps Institution of Oceanography have also been taking part in such studies as genetic variability, nearshore biotic communities, otter censusing, ecological energy-flow, feeding habits and food supply, behavioral repertoire, lung capacity and respiratory physiology, otter parasitology, the otter-kelp community, otter migration, causes of death, and Indian midden analysis.

AT UC SANTA CRUZ, Dr. John Pearse, during the winter of 1974-75, assigned his students to study and develop a "Formulation and Evaluation of a Policy on Sea Otters in California."

When students in this course wrote to Dr. Betty Davis for further information on the "conservationists' viewpoint and the ethics that led to that stand," she replied as follows:

"My own personal feeling is that a change is needed in human attitudes and values concerning wildlife. We must stop competing with nature and consider ourselves part of it before it is too late.

"My husband [Dr. John Davis, director of Hastings Natural History Reservation] and I view the otter-abalone-man conflict as a classic confrontation between man and beast—a real test case with man (not the otter) on trial! Here is an animal, the otter, just beginning to stabilize after a return from near extinction. It poses no threat to the continued existence of any resources—abalones, urchins, clams, crabs, or lobsters—as the otter's foraging does not eliminate breeding stocks.

"Will man, a top predator who does nothing to enhance the marine environment but much to deteriorate and exploit it, check his greed, examine his values, and allow a natural predator that belongs in and enhances this ecosystem go on its way without human interference? We believe this is a question of great import and significance to man at this critical time in his history.

"In summary, may I pose this question to you: At a time when we humans are just beginning to understand and appreciate the preciousness of all the environment and the interrelationships involving all living and nonliving portions of it, can we afford to risk manipulation of an important functioning element such as the southern sea otter, which is still making its way back from near extinction and whose important role in the nearshore marine environment is just beginning to become evident?"

ONE RESULT of all this academic scrutiny has been that the general public has been kept informed through the media whenever some new discovery has been brought to light, and that the otter has usually wound up as the beneficiary with more and more supporters rallying to its cause.

Lately, in addition to the threat from oil spills, much concern has been voiced about the dangers of water pollution through the release of sewage effluent at sea, and the high levels of poisonous metals such as cadmium, zinc, mercury, and lead in the otters' food. "Mercury," according to Dr. Mattison, "accumulates in food chains as a result of our continual use of fungicides, laundry bleaches, dental products, pool algacides, pesticides, and the processing of wood pulp, plastics, bleach, explosives, batteries, paint, cinnabar, lights, and electrical equipment." In addition to devouring marine life that may have absorbed some of these poisons, otters drink about two quarts of sea water per day.

Dr. James Rote, Commissioner of the Central California Coastal Commission, in his doctoral work at Hopkins Marine Station used otters to assess the levels of PCBs and DDE in Monterey Bay. Both of these cumulative toxicants were found in otter tissues.

A survey in 1975 by DFG biologist Michael Martin of copper discharge from the Diablo Cove nuclear power plant's cooling system is reported to have shown 4,185 dead abalones and 119,040 dead sea urchins in the cove. Copper was found in the tissues of representative samples. What effect this may have on sea otters is not known, but they were blamed during a hearing on the matter for wiping out the abalones. In a telegram sent for the record of the hearing, Dr. Betty Davis stated, among other things, that "otters foraging through an abalone bed don't leave copper-plated carcasses, they leave empty shells."

According to Jud Vandevere, between 50 and 60 dead otters were picked up along the central California coast during 1976. In tests made by Dr. John Martin of Moss Landing Marine Laboratories of body tissues sent to him by Vandevere, cadmium was the most significant of many metals discovered.

Chlordane used on shoreline golf courses drains directly into the ocean, Vandevere pointed out, with studies showing that DDE and DDD have been increasing 134 percent per year in the mud and sandy deposits of the bays, causing reproductive damage in sea lions, falcons, ospreys, and pelicans. Quoting Dr. John Phillips of Hopkins Marine Station, Vandevere said that it would take 10 years for the effects of the drainage of these derivatives of DDT to reach their peaks, so that the levels in otter tissues may increase during the next few years.

North of Big Sur where raw sewage used to flow into the ocean near an otter feeding place, "we found infectious lesions on otters that apparently interfered with their eating and caused their death," Mattison said.

Even the constant grooming of the fur is believed to pose dangers in polluted waters, as the otters thus ingest the chlorinated hydrocarbons and PCBs that have been washed into the sea.

THERE HAVE BEEN MANY LIGHTER MOMENTS during these research activities. Not all of them have been concerned with threats to the otter. Steven J. Shimek of UC Santa Cruz, writing in *The Otter Raft* about five weeks of underwater work trying to catch glimpses of how the otter obtains food, told of a large male otter off Cannery Row who "first called attention to himself by grabbing my leg underwater. He then swam a few feet away and began patting the sides of rocks, crevice depressions, and kelp holdfasts with his forepaws. From one holdfast he retrieved two small snails which he placed under his arm, resumed his patting of the substrate for approximately 15 seconds and then returned to the surface where we, remaining underwater, lost sight of him. . . .

"We observed an otter underwater in the harbor area of Stillwater Cove eating echiuroids—fat innkeepers, *Urechis caupo*—which are startling in appearance: pink, round worms, about an inch in diameter and about six inches in length, with golden bristles on both ends. They live in large U-shaped tubes burrowed in the mud. At the surface we were able to locate the otter's digging site because a thin stream of bubbles rose from the silty water below. While otters work underwater, air continuously escapes from their fur.

"When we descended to the otter's dig, we found ourselves facemask to face with the otter who, with his head turned to one side, was vigorously digging trenches in the silt and rocks in search of fat innkeepers."

Divers for the DFG have reported watching otters trying to dislodge food from underwater rocks and crevices and, when unable to do so, throwing rocks in an apparent pique, just as humans might do.

And Jud Vandevere has told of an otter that he saw vigorously waving a clump of the kelp known as "pom-pom" as if he were rooting at a football game.

Most of the herds remain wary of man, but individual animals, having satisfied themselves that they are not threatened, can seek attention and show off as readily as dogs, living up to their nicknames, "teddy bears of the sea," and "clowns of the kelp."

Female cradles two-week-old pup in her short forelimbs. Females with young pups tend to live away from other otters. (R. Buchsbaum)

14

BEHIND THE UNDERWATER LENS

A SURGEON AND AN ATTORNEY, both from Salinas, and both weekend sailing and scuba diving enthusiasts, have turned the underwater photography of sea otters into a fine art. It started when Dr. James A. Mattison, Jr., then living in Fresno, one of the hot spots of California's Central Valley, began coming to Monterey Peninsula to escape the heat.

"I kept seeing these strange animals out in the kelp and it became a challenge to get pictures of them," he said. So with both motion picture and still cameras he went to work, showing his first attempts to his friend William F. Bryan, who in true legal style began cross-examining him as to his aims and methods.

"Having flown a camera ship during World War II, I was sure I could do better than Jim, who knew that he could do better than Jud Vandevere, who knew he could do better than Karl Kenyon," said Bill Bryan.

Before long Bryan and Mattison were working out techniques together, sometimes aided by Vandevere. "We had been trying to get closeups for months," Bryan related the story. "The only one who was getting anything out of this was Eastman Kodak. We shot thousands of feet of their film. They should make a donation to Friends of the Sea Otter.

"Seen from underneath, an otter, to the cameraman, looks like a big brown bag hanging down in the water. But when we tried to get close enough for a head shot, the beasts would take off in fright, making a milkshake out of the water.

"One Sunday afternoon we were driving past Lovers Point, Pacific Grove, when we saw an otter diving for food, quite close

"Looks like a big brown bag," when seen from beneath by the photographer, is Bill Bryan's apt description of a sea otter descending to the bottom. (J.A. Mattison, Jr.)

to some people sitting on a rock. And the people didn't seem to bother the animal. We parked and struggled to climb into our wetsuits before this otter could get away. We both had motion picture cameras with 100-foot rolls in them. My camera had a bumper sticker, 'Ban the Draft,' pasted on the side. It was a sticker that Mrs. Vandevere had been distributing, this being during the days of our Southeast Asian involvement.

"Jim's camera had a parallax problem, though the system was supposedly very simple for adjusting the mechanism for closeups and distant shots. We shot our first 100 feet in no time, scrambled up the rocks back to the beach, up to the parking lot, unloaded, reloaded, and sent Mrs. Mattison into Monterey to buy more film. Have you ever tried to buy film in Monterey on a Sunday afternoon?

"Jim obtained some marvelous shots of the 'Ban the Draft' sticker on my camera. Nevertheless, we both got good footage of the otter. From that point on, we were hooked."

Their subjects, however, could be capricious, obstinate, uncooperative, and downright diabolical on occasion. When Bryan and Mattison learned that there was a raft of otters that had taken up residence near Hopkins Marine Station, they

Otters are curious. When alarmed by a diver's bubbles they first take evasive action, but then return to see what is going on. (Clark)

picked a sackful of sea urchins which they began to distribute in a large crack of an underwater rock frequented by the animals. The idea was to photograph the otters digging the urchins out of the crevice and eating them.

"We had a mesh nylon bag with a snap closure," said Mattison. "A lead weight held it on the bottom. But while we were taking urchins out to stuff into the rocky crack, otters grabbed the bag and swam off with the whole grocery store. A couple of other times they tore the bag apart to get at the contents."

On another occasion, Bryan had a bag of urchins and two underwater cameras, one of them weighing 85 pounds, tied together. An otter grabbed the rope and took the entire load to the surface.

One of the recurrent annoyances of underwater camera work being lack of sufficient light at critical moments, Bryan bought several hundred feet of cable and rented a 110-volt a.c. generator that he rigged on board his Boston whaler. He pounded metal stakes into underwater rocks in order to support the cable and 1,000-watt lamps, then placed food for the otters at strategic locations. The first otter to look into one of the lamps, however, twisted it around 180 degrees, then ran off with the sledge hammer and bag of food.

"Ron Church," said Mattison, "who was principal photographer on Cousteau's *The Unsinkable Sea Otter*, used to get his wife Joyce to sit on the bags of seafood at the bottom of the bay so that the otters couldn't make off with them. But in the reflection of Joyce's face mask, one of the animals could see what he thought was another otter. He ripped off the mask and carried it to the surface."

Mattison has owned various boats at different times, including a Thunderbird with twin outboards that kept getting caught in the kelp where the otters make their home. He substituted a pair of outboard jets that theoretically skim the water, but found them getting more entangled than ever.

Between the two of them, Bryan and Mattison have owned virtually a fleet, including a Chrysler outboard, an inflatable Zodiac with electric motor, a diesel-powered Baja 22, and the Boston whaler previously mentioned. They have sold and traded and replaced engines, and have towed one another from various points in Monterey Bay and along the central coast after motor failures. All of this has been in the interest of obtaining new, and characteristic, and appealing, and keenly interpretative pictures of otters, and of obtaining tidbits such as sea urchins to persuade their subjects to pose.

But at one point they decided that feeding the otters in order to photograph them was a questionable procedure. It resulted in the animals losing their timidity, becoming entirely tolerant of men and boats—with the eventual danger of their being cut by propellers and killed or maimed.

On the occasions when Bryan and Mattison could spend a few days at their underwater hobby, their procedure had been to spend the first two days visiting areas rich in otter food, and collecting enough for photographic purposes. The third day they "salted" the rocks where they planned to shoot.

Despite the otters' frequently making a fast grab for an urchin or abalone before cameras could be focused, the system on the whole worked very satisfactorily.

Diver offering a squid to an otter is overwhelmed with attention. Feeding of otters is discouraged because otters trained to come to human divers or boatmen will sooner or later get into trouble. (R. Church)

When otter bodies were occasionally found washed up on the beaches, showing slashes resembling propeller cuts, the two cameramen decided that their feeding routine must be discontinued. Some time afterwards, however, Jack Ames of the DFG, while examining slashes in dead otters, found fragments of teeth which he identified as those of a white shark. In some cases propellers were apparently not to blame. Nevertheless, as a matter of policy among Friends of the Sea Otter, feeding the animals has been stopped.

For the documentary film *Back from Extinction*, produced by Mattison with Bryan doing what Mattison refers to as "the lion's share of the photography," Bryan obtained, with Vandevere's assistance, some memorable footage of a mother otter sharing her food with her pup. Other sequences emphasize the otter's use of tools, such as using one Pismo clam as an anvil and another as a hammer. Vandevere said he still hopes to see photographed an

"Please don't feed the otters!" asks the Friends of the Sea Otter. Here an otter enthusiastically accepts a piece of squid, and in so doing is lured into focus for the photographer. "Freeloading" makes otters unwary of the dangers of boats and their sharp propellers and attracts otters to the polluted waters near wharves and marinas. (R. Buchsbaum)

exhibit of dexterity which he witnessed of an otter using its paws to twist a clam shell open without breaking the shell.

Mattison said that in addition to seeing otters "drinking" young octopuses out of discarded beer cans, he had seen them breaking coke bottles with a rock in order to get at the octopuses inside, or to get at clams that had grown inside the bottle and become too large to get out through the neck.

At the boat launching ramp at the Monterey marina, he said, he had watched a large male otter dining on gaper and Washington clams. "If they can get hold of the base of the gaper's siphon," he remarked, "they'll dig like mad to bring up the entire clam."

As experts in the life habits of the sea otter, Mattison and Bryan, along with Vandevere, have frequently been called on to reunite pups that have been separated from their mothers.

"One night," related Vandevere, "a bitch police dog brought into the kitchen of a house at Yankee Point a live baby sea otter. I was called and I got in touch with Warren Smith, the DFG warden, and Dr. Ronald Branson, a Monterey pediatrician, who whipped up a special formula for feeding the tiny creature—cod liver oil and whipped cream were the principal ingredients, if I remember correctly. Bill Bryan drove out to assist us in getting the pup back into the water."

Bryan took up the story: "It was still pitch dark when we stumbled down the rocky path to the beach. Some big guy came out of a nearby house and yelled 'What are you doing trespassing?' Warren Smith had to show him his badge before he could be convinced that we weren't malefactors of some kind. Finally I waded out through the surf and put the pup in the ocean. For the next several days Jud Vandevere kept watch but never saw a pup's dead body, so we assumed that its mother had reclaimed it."

On another occasion, said Vandevere, a pup was washed ashore at Wildcat Cove. DFG officials, dubious about the possibilities of reuniting it, insisted on taking it to a zoo in San Jose. A resident of the Wildcat Cove area, Mrs. John McDaniel, reported hearing an otter (possibly the mother) crying all night, Vandevere said.

During the Alaskan translocation of otters to areas where it was hoped to establish new rafts, one female drowned, leaving a pup that was picked up by another female that had lost a pup, Dr. Mattison reported. "There's always a good chance of an adoption in the natural environment, which is another reason for returning stranded pups to the sea near the spot where they were found," he declared.

As an illustration of the great attachment between female otters and pups, Vandevere cited the fact that he had seen a mother otter offshore from Presidio Curve tending her dead pup for three days, and on another occasion had seen a female treating a dead bird as if it were a pup.

During the filming of the Cousteau feature, *The Unsinkable Sea Otter,* Bryan, Vandevere, and Mattison were called on to lend their expertise as consultants. This was during the days in 1970-1971 when they were still feeding their own photographic subjects, so they suggested to the members of the French diving team that they get some abalones but warned them about taking only those of legal size.

"A warden in Santa Cruz phoned me," said Mattison, "to report that he had picked up a group of Frenchmen with 20 undersized abalones. They had referred him to me. Otherwise, on that particular day they spoke no English. Fortunately I was able to persuade the warden that they did not fully understand our laws."

Called also as consultants by a Stanford Research Institute unit that had two otters at Pigeon Point, which seemingly were not thriving though fed an ample diet of fish, Bryan and Mattison decided that the diet was incorrect. Bryan, with his son Bill, Jr., Mattison, and Vandevere took his inflatable Zodiac to nearby Año Nuevo Island, dived for abalones, and brought them to Pigeon Point. "The otters perked up immediately," he said.

"I learned there," he added, "that an otter can handle two

Sea otter foraging on bottom is briefly distracted by the photographer from its routine of "padding" the rocks and crevices with forepaws or exploring rocky surfaces with stout whiskers. Otters appear to pay no attention to bat stars *(Patiria),* of which three can be seen on the bottom at left, but they do feed on some species of sea stars. (J.A. Mattison, Jr.)

legal-sized abalones at a meal, but not three. A third is too much."

More recently, Bryan received a phone call from Tokyo wanting to know if he could assist a Japanese film crew in obtaining sea otter footage. "Certainly," he replied. How about a white-faced otter, he was asked. "Yes," he answered. How about a white-faced otter eating a clam? "That could be arranged," he said.

Within a day or two the Japanese film crew arrived in Monterey, met Bryan, and with his help shot 5,000 feet of film.

"It was to be edited for a 10-second television commercial," he said.

There was an 18-month period during which Vandevere closely followed the activities of an otter that "hauled out" almost nightly onto the beach in a rocky cove at Hopkins Marine Station. Easily identifiable by a triangular pattern of white on its head, it came ashore usually between 4 and 5 p.m., moving up the beach as the tide came in. At about 5 a.m. it returned to the water.

This was the first instance of regular hauling out that had come to the attention of otter-watchers on the Monterey Peninsula, so Jud frequently camped out with a sleeping bag in an effort to determine whether the animal followed an identical routine each night. Though he could almost touch it on occasion, he was careful to remain just far enough away so as not to alarm it or interact with it in any way, and often lay on the rocks just above the beach trying to remain concealed while keeping an eye on its movements. Bill Bryan, alerted to its presence, was able to move in close enough for some excellent photographs.

At one of the periodic open houses held for the public at the marine station, a division of the Department of Biological Sciences of Stanford University, Vandevere had seen the otter coming ashore. He asked the visitors to back away from the beach area, but to a point where they could still see the animal, whose arrival proved the highlight of the day.

The audience was convinced that this had been especially planned for its benefit. As a result, a newspaper columnist nicknamed the animal "Hopkins," by which it was known for as long as it continued to appear. Jud discovered, however, that its arrivals and departures were not entirely predictable. During the November-December and June-July periods it failed to show up in the area. Since these are peak times for sexual activity among the otters, Jud decided that Hopkins was probably going back into the range for mating purposes.

He also became convinced that Hopkins was able to sniff him out when the two were near one another in the cove, but that the otter had become accustomed to having a human nearby and felt no threat.

One of Vandevere's self-imposed chores during the 18-month period of the animal's visits was to collect its waste products in order to determine what it had been eating. "I had to spend days cataloging my findings and also washing out the containers, usually yogurt cartons," he said. "One day the station director had decided that faculty and students should have a noontime picnic. My cartons were monopolizing the principal table.

"Dr. Donald Abbott, one of the professors, seeing my yogurt containers, decided that this was a good place to bring his lunch. He was more than a little surprised when he saw the contents."

As a result of his examinations of the feces, which contained more than 40 different types of food remains, Jud categorized the otter as an "opportunistic" feeder taking whatever is available in the marine environment, from tiny crabs to abalones. Meanwhile his wife Joyce became accustomed to having his samples of evidence stored in the family freezer.

As a further example of the opportunistic feeding, Dr. Donald Abbott at Hopkins Marine Station discovered that the massive mussel beds, which had been a feature of the offshore rocks, had suddenly decreased, reduced by a raft of otters.

Though Hopkins, the only otter known to have been studied continuously in the wild for 18 months, was also the first southern sea otter known to have made hauling out a nightly ritual, others have since been discovered from time to time at Cypress Point Golf Club on a seaweed-covered rock visible from the 17th tee. And a pair were noted coming ashore at Fan Shell Beach on the 17-Mile Drive. They seem to haul out where they apparently feel safe from human interference.

More recently, graduate students at U.C. Santa Cruz have reporting seeing as many as 23 hauled out along one waterfront area.

One male, given the name of Angus, had a favorite place to come ashore at Otter Point south of Carmel, where he frequently persuaded a female to join him. He was captured there and tagged, which permitted metabolic studies to be made for a couple of weeks, since Angus cooperated by remaining where observations could be continued.

IN THE ONLY SUCCESSFUL COURT PROSECUTION on record since 1911 of a person or persons accused of killing sea otters, Vandevere, Mattison, and Bryan played significant roles in obtaining a conviction, though they give the major credit to the prompt response of the State Department of Fish and Game.

The incident began at Cambria May 25, 1970, where residents heard shots offshore and then saw an individual aboard a commercial abalone boat firing into a group of sea otters in the water. Immediately recognizing this as an illegal act, the witnesses to the shooting called the DFG in Morro Bay, which sent out a patrol boat. Upon its approach, the abalone boat took off at top speed for its home port, also Morro Bay, with the patrol boat in hot pursuit. At the entrance to the bay the gun was thrown overboard, but DFG divers, in cold, rough and murky water, retrieved it.

On the deck of the abalone boat spent cartridges were found, matching those still in the gun. DFG wardens picked up three dead otters from a Cambria kelp bed and took them to Salinas where, at Salinas Valley Memorial Hospital, Dr. Mattison and Vandevere took x-rays, located the bullets, and recovered them, being very careful not to scratch them. (The hospital, said Mattison, has been very helpful in permitting the use of x-ray and other facilities in otter necropsies.)

Test rounds were fired from the gun to compare ballistics. The bullets matched exactly, establishing a chain of evidence. It was determined that the gun had been purchased in Morro Bay by the owner of the abalone boat. Calling in attorney Bryan for professional advice, Mattison and Vandevere wrote a report as a scientific and legal document, prepared so that it could be presented in a court of law. It was sent to the DFG in Sacramento.

Trial was set in Morro Bay, where Mrs. Mattison's mother found herself seated next to one of the accused. "Actually a very likeable chap," said Dr. Mattison. "He came to visit us later to find out what our attitude was with respect to otters. To him, they were just animals competing for his livelihood. He was one of three convicted, given a $1,000 fine and one year in jail (suspended). The three were allowed one year to raise the $1,000 each, but their abalone licenses were suspended."

The one other otter shooting case that went to court ran into a legal roadblock, said Vandevere.

Jud and Dr. Michael McRoberts had gone to the Pacific Gas and Electric Company's nuclear power plant at Diablo Canyon, he related, and were in the north cove "surrounded by Pinkerton police who insisted that we wear bright yellow hard hats," when they heard shooting and saw an abalone boat, which took off as soon as its occupants noted the yellow hats and knew that they had been seen. At Jud's insistence, the DFG was radioed and it attempted to make an interception.

Hours later, Jud found an otter carcass in the water, which DFG Capt. Hugh Thomas recovered for him. "It had been shot and had drowned," Jud said. "I had one of Jim Mattison's garbage cans in the back of my car, so I drove to Avila, filled it with ice, and took the carcass to Salinas, where Dr. Mattison, Dr. McRoberts, Dr. Betty Davis, Jack Ames, and I necropsied it. It was full of shotgun pellets. Again we started to establish a chain of evidence, but no ballistics can be proved on shotgun pellets, and the gun was not recovered.

"The U.S. attorney ordered us to appear before a grand jury in Los Angeles, where we were asked to identify the abalone boat captain in a police lineup. This was obviously impossible, as we had seen the boat itself only from a distance. That was the last we ever heard of the case."

THOUGH *Homo sapiens* has been the predator most responsible for the threatened state of the sea otter, there have been otters that have developed quite an affinity for humans, according to Vandevere, Mattison, and Bryan. "One of the Cousteau diving team's favorite subjects was an animal with a sort of silver cape," recalled Bryan. "But if they wanted special footage of it, they had to rely on one diver-cameraman, Jacqui. This otter liked Jacqui and would come at once when it saw him. Why? Who knows? Just the way dogs and cats seem to have an instant rapport with some people and are indifferent to others."

15

WHAT NEXT?

THOUGH the sea otters themselves were given no opportunity to express an opinion on their latest status and life style, some 67,000 citizens across the U.S. had signed petitions and almost 300 had written letters urging their "threatened" classification and opposing range restriction. Presumably as many or more citizens would be watching the translocation experiments with keen interest. Two of the letters were document-sized efforts by the FSO and the Sierra Club.

WHEN THE Alaska Department of Fish and Game was trying to repopulate some of the Aleutian Islands with otters after the Amchitka blast, Carl Schneider, noting that the animals were swimming all around him and had already found their way to these islands, made a remark that has since been frequently repeated: "No matter what we plan for the otters, they'll manage their own affairs."

It remains to be seen how the California sea otters react to any proposal to manage their affairs for them, but when this book went to press a few of them were already sighted off Santa Barbara, and a Malibu resident, John Vogler, had written to *The Otter Raft* describing his adventures with two otters off Point Dume, one a female that stayed about a month, the other a male, nicknamed Oscar, that remained about a year.

"We miss Oscar, as he became part of our lives," Vogler wrote. "I would play with him almost every day when he came in from his kelp bed to feed. I would go down on the beach and wave my fins at him and he would come roaring in so that by the time I was in the water with fins on, he would be there ready for fun. We had water acrobatics together ... snuggling up his face under my chin with me scratching his chest. We had all-out diving attacks and I have the scars to prove it, since he did not realize that my 'paws' were not as tough as his. On two occasions, he swam along with me for quite a distance (once over half a mile). Swimming on his back, he had to slow down considerably to keep me company. When I would swim to the outer kelp bed where he was sleeping, wrapped in his blanket of kelp, he would pay no attention at all—other than lazily opening one eye about half way.

"We did not feed Oscar at any time, but got him used to us by simply 'doing his thing'—rolling over, rubbing our 'fur,' back-swimming, and always only saying one sound, 'hello Oscar.' He was lonely, I think."

There was a sequel to the Oscar story. The Voglers visited Monterey during their vacation and were taken on a tour of otter-viewing spots by Jud Vandevere, who explained his research work and experiments. After they returned to Malibu, daughter Lynn Vogler wrote:

"Oscar returned for two days carrying on his same old routine and behavior. During that time we watched him playing with a seal about 50 feet offshore for about two to three hours. He seemed to lead the seal around in their playful water acts. This seemed very unusual to us and we wondered if this was quite a common thing. It seems Oscar has extended his range 3-4 miles south of us now. We are certainly very happy to see him and to know that he is still around."

HOW LONG Oscar and his relatives will be around apparently depends upon a complex of many factors, some of them very unfriendly to otters. Even the protection of the Endangered Species Act appears to be a sometime thing. In October 1978 the agency charged with enforcing the act suddenly closed its office because the Congress had not renewed its funding. The Act was subsequently reauthorized with weakening amendments, and the office reopened for 18 months. But there are new hazards in the offing.

In addition to the threat of tanker spills, there is the probability of oil drilling off the central California coast; and bidding for offshore tracts is scheduled to be opened in that area by the U.S. Department of the Interior in a year or two. Environmentalists forsee the likelihood of a repetition of the drilling leaks or blow-out experienced in the Santa Barbara Channel if the leases are approved, equipment installed, and pumping begun.

Organizations such as Ventana chapter of the Sierra Club have petitioned the National Oceanic and Atmospheric Administration to designate Monterey Bay from Año Nuevo Island to Point Sur as a federal marine sanctuary. Such designation could protect vital marine and coastal resources, fragile wildlife habitat areas, unique wildlife populations, including otters, and an entire and complex marine ecosystem which includes the kelps and many sport and commercial fishes that appear to be favored by the presence of otters.

Creation of a federal marine sanctuary would also preclude ocean mining and dredging operations, and dumping of agricultural and industrial wastes and sewage effluent, all of which either have been or could be harmful to otters—not to mention all marine life. The Sierra Club petition further pointed out that although the California sea otter is presumably protected by the Endangered Species Act and the Marine Mammal Protection Act, the animal and its habitat are not protected against oil development and other sources of pollution.

In July 1978, the California Coastal Commission recommended to the federal government that a proposed lease sale of off-shore drilling sites be suspended until there is evidence that such drilling would not harm the environment. This recommendation went unheeded, and by fall the Bureau of Land Management had accepted nominations and selected 5 areas of high interest for further environmental study, requiring that an Environmental Impact Statement (EIS) be made. Since two of the high interest areas are at the northern and southern ends of the otter's range, conservationists fear that spilled oil could be widely dispersed and destroy the entire southern sea otter population.

SEATED at her desk in the new Sea Otter Center at the Barnyard at the entrance to Carmel Valley, Margaret Owings interrupted her work on *The Otter Raft.* "You ask me what is next for Friends of the Sea Otter?" she laughed. "We hardly have time to make future plans! Actually, we move with the tides. We are kept busy responding to constant efforts on the part of the DFG to undo whatever protection we have thus far won for the otters."

"For a decade, we've feared an oil-spill, such as the one this spring of the American-owned supertanker, the *Amoco Cadiz,* off the Brittany coast, the fourth bad oil spill on that coast in eleven years, and so far the most catastrophic of all oil spills anywhere in the world. It may take 10 years or more to remove the effects on a stretch of coast that supplies one-third of all the shellfish in France.

"We've been pushing for translocation of otters to form new separate colonies such as along a coastal stretch to the north of the state and an island to the south. But the U.S. Supreme Court recently transferred the waters around Anacapa and Santa Barbara Islands in the Channel Islands National Monument from federal to state control. Though many sea mammals are on these islands, and otters were originally abundant there, it would appear that in the eyes of the DFG, the otters are not now welcome. Limited abalone harvesting is still taking place and there is no room for otters there in DFG plans for the future.

"In addition, the Outer Continental Shelf Oil-Drilling (Lease #53) could present a very serious threat to the otters since it embraces, in totality, their present range. Yet, the DFG biologists have devoted themselves almost single-mindedly to restricting the spread of the sea otters along the coast of California. *The Sun Bulletin,* Morro Bay, June 15, 1978, quotes one of the DFG biologists as saying, 'The only way to control the sea otter population in California is to remove the status of the sea otter under the 1972 Endangered Species Act.' By relocating them and removing the protection of the Act, he claimed, 'hopefully, we can save the shellfish fisheries.'

"At the same time that comment was made, we received notice through the *Federal Register* that the southern sea otter is proposed for a change in listing, from Appendix I to Appendix II, of the Convention on International Trade in Endangered Species. Such a change could weaken the protection of sea otters from future trade in otter pelts.

"The legal status of the sea otter is continually changing and we are continually dealing with the same DFG philosophy that places the harvestable shellfish (for which licenses are purchased) at the top of the list while the little otter, which is not a hunter's trophy, is categorized primarily as a 'predator.'

"This trim little Otter Center," Margaret remarked, looking around with pride, at the photographs, drawings, books, and otter objects, "is an illustration of an immense and growing human interest in the otters themselves. We have thousands of members, not only from California but from almost every state in the Union and across the seas. People seek us out, asking for information. They come from Sweden, from Switzerland, from England, writing ahead to ask for our help in taking them out to see the otters! They come from New York, Florida, Wisconsin, and of course, they come from California. The otter is becoming the insignia for motels, travel agencies, restaurants, and gift shops. The most common question asked at the entrance to Point Lobos State Park is 'Where can we see the otters?' The DFG might well focus attention on this enthusiastic portion of the public! Watching otters is a unique delight, and a new form of recreation. But alas," she said sadly, "the otter-watchers don't buy licenses from the DFG—and that's a factor, apparently, that counts."

AT HIS OFFICE in the California Department of Fish and Game, headquarters in Monterey, Dan Miller, the state's most vigorous DFG spokesman, says that he is really trying to have a balanced viewpoint. "I realize we have the responsibility of writing rules to protect all of the state's resources; we must recognize legitimate claims of every group, and we cannot favor one over another.

"We firmly believe that sea otters living in known abalone or clam fishing grounds preclude a commercial or sports fishery for these shellfish. We, therefore, feel we have a complex and difficult task. We have to know a great deal about the marine ecosystem including plankton, kelp, sea urchins, abalones, fishes, and sea otters, not to mention many other marine organisms. And we must control the sea otter as well as protect it. The people of the state must make the final decision—what do they want most?"

BIOLOGICAL SCIENTIST, Dr. Ralph Buchsbaum, responding to my query about the future of marine resources, turned philosophical. "Perhaps you should put me down as an optimist in these matters. We optimists are those who still think the future is *uncertain!* We refuse to believe that *all* humans lack the intelligence and the will to reverse the degradation of water quality and the overfishing that is causing catastrophic declines in both fish and shellfish yields not just in California but around the world. In some areas the yields are rising because of improved technology, but this only hastens the final 'crash.'

"I like to cite bits of happy news like the return of some fishes to certain cleaned-up rivers. But at present the bright spots are few. In 1950 I attended a seminar at which the leading statistician of the British fisheries assured his audience of biologists that (though bottom fishes were declining) the herring—historically a staple food in much of Europe—was in no danger because fishermen could not overexploit fishes with pelagic breeding habits. Sonar technology applied to fishing changed all that, and today the herring is all but wiped out—a catastrophe on a scale that can hardly be appreciated by an American diver hunting abalones for a few diners in expensive restaurants or merely for recreation.

"Returning to Thailand in 1970, after an absence of ten years, I found that the human population had risen from 22 million to 28 million, but that the huge estuarine prawns on which so many people depended, and which I had enjoyed almost daily for a year, were down to less than half the 1960 yield.

"At Lewes, on Delaware Bay, where I used to take my classes to see the riches of marine life, industrial pollution has taken a fearful toll. But even so, it was overfishing that had caused the large local menhaden fleet to try their luck on other shores and other fishes. The million-dollar oyster industry closed down too—no minor loss to a small fishing town. Now Lewes has a busy establishment of biologists trying to learn how to bring back the fishes, and a large mariculture project that is having success in growing oysters in unpolluted tanks on land.

"It all comes down to what Garrett Hardin has so aptly called *The Tragedy of the Commons.* In past centuries many towns had a commons—a publicly owned grassy plot, often in the center of town, on which any citizen could pasture cows. It worked out well as long as each person acted responsibly. The system broke down when the number of people and their cows increased, and some individuals began to overload the commons, pasturing more than their fair share of cows. Those who were the least considerate reaped the most benefits. There was no incentive, as with the private ownership of land, to limit one's demands on the land in order to maintain a continuing bounty for one's self and one's descendants.

"The oceans are a commons. The natural resources that belong to everyone—therefore to no one—can survive only if every individual shares the commons responsibly. To quote Hardin again, in *Stalking the Wild Taboo:* '... in a world of less than perfect human beings—and we will never know any other— mutual ruin is inevitable in the commons!'

"A marine ecosystem, developed over millions of years, by natural selection of plant and animal populations that are well adapted to the physical conditions and to each other, is not likely to be improved by uninformed tinkering. And certainly not by citizens going to the ballot box to vote for abalone dinners.

"The relationships between kelps, sea urchins, crabs, abalones, and sea otters—to mention only a few—are so complex they have been studied for years by biologists in the DFG and in the universities without yielding all the information needed to "manage" these marine resources with confidence that human interference will do more good than harm. The problem of an expanding human population trying to draw ever-increasing yields of fishes or shellfish from a marine environment that is being rapidly degraded has been faced realistically in some parts of the world. In California the DFG, pressured by demanding licencees, is using the promise of restriction of the sea otter as a means of mollifying its diving clientele and of putting off the evil day when the DFG will have to explain the painful facts of over-exploitation to the citizens of California.

"The future of sea otters is still uncertain. At least for the next few years, I would restrict and regulate supertankers and abalonetakers, but not otters. I would keep supertankers out of Monterey Bay, and oil-rigs away from the Monterey and Santa Cruz County coasts. I would urge the citizens to focus their attention on protecting California shores from sewage, toxic chemicals, and oil. I hope the DFG will have the funds to continue its field and laboratory studies, and its cooperation with university biologists, but I would also ask the DFG to discourage the anti-otter extremists among the abalone divers. Their right to kill and eat abalones is no greater than mine to enjoy seeing abalones in the rock crevices and sea otters in the kelp beds. I would encourage efforts to develop mariculture of abalones and other molluscs as a highly probable solution for meeting indefinitely expanding demands for shellfish (witness the growth of the chicken, turkey, and commercial mushroom industries). I would ask the Friends of the Sea Otter to maintain vigilance over the quality of life for all shore inhabitants. And when they are not fighting to prevent their past efforts from being undone, I hope they will have the energy to help the DFG get direct state funding so as to be more free of economic pressures when they make biological decisions.

"Nature has remarkable recuperative powers, as we can see in the return of the California sea otter from a small remnant. But there is much evidence that both plant and animal populations that make a comeback from a small number of individuals inevitably suffer a great loss of the genetic variability needed to respond adaptively to changing conditions. The otter population, after an early rapid expansion, appears now to be stabilizing. It could even be decreasing, for all we know; the last census was in 1976. The most choice otter prey, that grew unchecked in the absence of predation, are fewer now and closer to the more natural balance that existed in the past, while many of the kinds of small animals eaten by otters must benefit from the increased growth of kelp. If we are entering a period of massive oil spills and drilling leaks, no animal population on this coast is as clearly vulnerable as is the sea otter. So predictions are chancy. Nevertheless, there are many sound biological reasons for supposing that shore waters in which the sea otters can survive will also provide best for humans who live along such a shore. Is it too optimistic to believe that enough Californians will understand this and act on it?"

IN 1973 Gerald Durrell, noted British zoologist who has authored *A Zoo in My Luggage* and *The Whispering Land* among other books of adventure on the world's nature trails, came to Monterey to see Cannery Row and the sea otters. "Sure enough," he wrote, "there were all the settings for Steinbeck's book, it was marvelous to see. What I also wanted particularly to see there were the sea otters, the subspecies which has just reappeared in that area. I was taken out in a little boat and there were the California sea lions sitting on the breakwater honking at us, then after about five minutes we came to the kelp beds, those extraordinary seaweed beds that are so long, glossy and thick, and there in these kelp beds were all the sea otters carefully wrapped up as though they were in bed, all lying on their backs in the water with their heads sticking up and their paws together. They looked like a convention of bishops in mud baths in Baden Baden or somewhere like that. They are quite the most enchanting animals I think I have ever seen."

(J.A. Mattison, Jr.)

THE FRIENDS OF THE SEA OTTER, which means virtually everyone who has laid eyes on this doughty denizen of the near-shore deep, heartily endorse this sentiment. And the DFG has been given the responsibility for protecting this animal that now has become a "growth industry" in California.

SO WHAT MORE can be said, except a parting salutation to the otter from California author Wallace Stegner: "This is to wish you happiness—a nice rocking kelp bed, a rock on your stomach, an abalone on the rock, and a row of admiring spectators on your cliff."

Selected Readings

Articles and Books of General Interest

Costa, Daniel. The Sea Otter. Its Interaction with Man. *Oceanus* **21**(2):24-30. 1978.

Davis, Betty S. The Southern Sea Otter Revisited. *Pacific Discovery* **30**(2):1-13. 1977.

Duplaix-Hall, Nicole. Otters of the World. *Animals* **14**(10):438-442. 1972.

Fitch, John E. *The Pismo Clam.* Marine Resources Leaflet No. 1, The Resources Agency, Calif. Dept. Fish and Game. 1977.

Haley, D., ed. *Marine Mammals of Eastern North Pacific and Arctic Waters.* Seattle: Pacific Search Press. 1978.

Hunt, William R. *Arctic Passage. The Turbulent History of the Land and People of the Bering Sea, 1697-1975.* New York: Scribners. 1975.

Kenyon, Karl W. Return of the Sea Otter. With photographs by James A. Mattison, Jr. *National Geographic* : 520-539. October 1971.

Kenyon, Karl W. *The Sea Otter in the Eastern Pacific Ocean.* New York: Dover Publications. 1975.

MacLeish, William H., ed. Oil in Coastal Waters. *Oceanus* **20**(4):2-94. 1977.

Martin, Fredericka. *Sea Bears. The Story of the Fur Seal* [and other sea mammals]. Philadelphia: Chilton Company. 1960.

Miller, D. J. *The Sea Otter, Enhydra lutris.* Marine Resources leaflet No. 7. Resources Agency, California Department Fish and Game. 1974.

Ogden, Adele. *The California Sea Otter Trade, 1784-1848.* Berkeley: University of California Press. 1941.

Palmer, L. W. The Otter Slaughter. *Oceans* **4**(6):28-33. 1971.

Palmisano, John F., and James A. Estes. Sea Otters: Pillars of the Nearshore Community. *Natural History* **85**(7):46-52. Aug.-Sept. 1976.

Sedgwick, Dan. Replanting the Ocean Garden. Abalone Farming off Santa Barbara. *Oceans* **4**:61-62. 1978.

Technical Articles and Reports

Barabash-Nikiforov, I. I. *The Sea Otter.* Translated from Russian by A. Birron and Z. S. Cole, for the National Science Foundation, Washington, D.C., by the Israel Program for Scientific Translations, Jerusalem, Israel. 1962.

Bigg, Michael A., and Ian B. MacAskie. Sea Otters Reestablished in British Columbia. *Journal Mammology* **59**(4):874-876. 1978.

Bonnot, P. The Abalones of California. *California Fish and Game* **34**(4):141-168. 1948.

Burge, S., S. A. Schultz, and M. W. Odemar. Draft report on recent abalone research in California with recommendations for management. Operations Resources Branch and Mar. Resources Regions. State of Calif. Resource Agency. California Dept. Fish and Game. 1975.

Cicin-Sain, B., J. E. Moore, and A. J. Wyner. *Management Approaches for Marine Fisheries: The Case of the California Abalone.* Institute of Marine Resources, University of California, La Jolla. 1977.

Cooper, J., M. Wieland, and A. Hines. Subtidal abalone populations in an area inhabited by sea otters. *Veliger* **20**(2):163-169. 1977.

Costa, Daniel P. The Ecological Energetics, Water and Electrolyte Balance of the California Sea Otter, *Enhydra lutris.* Ph.D. thesis, University of California, Santa Cruz. 1978.

Davis, J., and W. Z. Lidicker, Jr. The Taxonomic Status of the Southern Sea Otter. *Proc. California Academy of Sciences* **40**(14):429-437. 1975.

Dayton, Paul K. Experimental studies of algal canopy interactions in a sea otter-dominated kelp community at Amchitka Island, Alaska. United States National Marine Fisheries Service Fishery Bulletin **73**:230-237. 1975.

Ebert, Earl E. *Foraging Activity of Sea Otters in the San Simeon-Cambria Region.* The Resource Agency, California Department of Fish and Game, Marine Resources Operations, Reference No. 67-31. 1967.

Ebert, Earl E. A Food Habits Study of the Southern Sea Otter, *Enhydra lutris nereis. Calif. Fish & Game* **54**:33-42. 1968.

Estes, J. A., and J. F. Palmisano. Sea Otters: Their Role in Structuring Nearshore Communities. *Science* **185**:1058-1060. 1974.

Estes, J. A., N. Smith, and J. F. Palmisano. Sea Otter Predation and Community Organization in the Western Aleutian Islands, Alaska. *Ecology* **59**(4):822-833. 1978.

Faro, James B. A Survey of Subtidal Sea Otter Habitat off Point Pinos, California. M.S. thesis, Humboldt State College. 1969.

Harris, Robert K. Feeding and Other Activities of the Sea Otter, *Enhydra lutris,* along Cannery Row, Monterey, California. B.A. thesis in Environmental Studies, Crown College, University of California, Santa Cruz. 1977.

Loughlin, Thomas R. Activity Patterns, Habitat Partitioning, and Grooming Behavior of the Sea Otter, *Enhydra lutris,* in California. Ph.D. thesis, University of California, Los Angeles. 1977.

Lowry, F. L., and Pearse, J. S. Abalones and Sea Urchins in an Area Inhabited by Sea Otters. *Marine Biology* **23**:213-219. 1973.

Miller, Daniel., and J. J. Geibel. *Summary of Blue Rockfish and Lingcod Life Histories; a Reef Ecology Study; and Giant Kelp, Macrocystis pyrifera Experiments in Monterey Bay, California.* Resources Agency, California Dept. Fish and Game. Fish Bulletin 158. 1973.

Miller, Daniel J., James E. Hardwick, and Walter A. Dahlstrom. *Pismo Clams and Sea Otters.* Marine Resources Technical Report No. 13. 1975.

Morejohn, G. Victor, Jack A. Ames, and David B. Lewis. *Post Mortem Studies of Sea Otters, Enhydra lutris L., in California.* Marine Resources Technical Report No. 30. 1975.

Mottet, Madelon G. *A Review of the Fishery Biology of Abalones.* State of Washington Dept. Fisheries. Technical Report No. 37. 1978.

Operations Research Branch. *A Proposal for Sea Otter Protection and Research and Request for the Return of Management to the State of California.* California Department of Fish and Game. 1976.

Pearse, John S., and Lowry, Lloyd F., eds. An Annotated Species List of the Benthic Algae and Invertebrates in the Kelp Forest Community at Point Cabrillo, Pacific Grove, Calif. Technical Report No. 1. Coastal Marine Laboratory, University of California, Santa Cruz. 1974.

Roest, A. I. Subspecies of the sea otter, *Enhydra lutris. Los Angeles County, Nat. Hist. Mus., Contrib. Sci.* **252**:1-17. 1973.

Sandegrew, F. E., E. W. Chu, and J. E. Vandevere. Maternal Behavior in California Sea Otter. *J. Mamm.* **54**(3):668-679. 1973.

Shimek, S. J., and A. Monk. Daily Activities of Sea Otters off Monterey Peninsula, California. *Jour. of Wildlife Management* **41**(2):277-283. 1977.

Simenstad, C. A., J. A. Estes, and K. W. Kenyon. Aleuts, Sea Otters, and Alternate Stable-State Communities. *Science* **200**:403-411. 1978.

Todd, Ethel, and Karl Kenyon. Selected Bibliography on the Sea Otter. Fish and Wildlife Service. Special Scientific Report. Wildlife No. 149. 1972.

Wild, R. W., and J. A. Ames. A Report on the Sea Otter, *Enhydra lutris L.,* in California. Calif. Dept. Fish & Game, Mar. Res. Tech. Report **20**:1-93. 1974.

Woodhouse, Charles D., Jr., Robert K. Cowen, and Larry Wilcoxon. *A Summary of Knowledge of the Sea Otter, Enhydra lutris L., in California and an Appraisal of the Completeness of Biological Understanding of the Species.* Santa Barbara Mus. Nat. Hist. Report prepared for the Marine Mammal Commission, Washington, D.C. 1976.

Yellin, Marc B., Catherine R. Agegian, and John S. Pearse. *Ecological Benchmarks in the Santa Cruz County Kelp Forests before the Re-establishment of Sea Otters.* Technical Report No. 6. Center for Coastal Marine Studies, University of California, Santa Cruz. 1977.

INDEX